PARLEY'S PRIMARY HISTORIES.

A

HISTORY OF ASIA

AND

OCEANICA.

By S. G. GOODRICH,
AUTHOR OF PETER PARLEY'S TALES.

PUBLISHED BY
MORTON AND GRISWOLD,
LOUISVILLE, KY.
1850.

REVISED COMPREHENSIVE READERS;

S. G. GOODRICH.

☞ The series of Comprehensive Readers has been carefully revised, and is much improved and enlarged, containing numerous new and appropriate engravings. A new *First Reader* has been added, making the set now complete. It is as follows:—

The First School Reader ...... *by* S. G. GOODRICH.
The Second School Reader ..... *by* S. G. GOODRICH.
The Third School Reader ..... *by* S. G. GOODRICH.
The Fourth School Reader ..... *by* S. G. GOODRICH.
The Fifth School Reader ... .. *by* S. G. GOODRICH.

COMPLETE SERIES OF PRIMARY HISTORIES.

BY S. G. GOODRICH.

☞ This series comprises the following works:—

1. *History of North America.*
2. *History of South America and the West Indies.*
3. *History of Europe.*
4. *History of Africa.*
5. *History of Asia and Oceanica.*

These works are specially designed for common schools and families. They comprise an entertaining and instructive view of Universal History.

Entered, according to Act of Congress, in the year 1850,
BY S. G. GOODRICH,
In the Clerk's Office of the District Court of Massachusetts.

PREFACE.

The following, which forms the preface to the History of North America, will explain the purpose of this volume, and constitute a proper introduction to the same:—

"The author of this little book has been requested to prepare a series of Histories, of such simplicity in style and arrangement, as to make them suitable *books for beginners*. The present volume has been written in compliance with this request, and with the hope of rendering it proper as an introduction to the study of history, especially in our common schools.

"Notwithstanding the numerous books upon this subject, it is still matter of fact that thousands of schools in the country have not yet introduced the study of history; and the reason assigned is, that no suitable book is found, to be put into the hands of young pupils—those who have everything upon the subject of history yet to learn.

"This volume is prepared in view of this state of things, and it is hoped it may attain the object at which it aims. It is designed to be the first of a series; the whole to form a simple outline of general history. The succeeding volumes will embrace South America, Europe, Asia, and Africa."

This series is now complete, and forms an outline of Universal History, in five volumes, illustrated by engravings and maps, and rendered attractive as far as possible, by introducing the more agreeable as well as instructive portions of history, such as the progress of society, the manners and customs of different ages and countries, and the lives of eminent characters—all tending to unfold the designs of Providence in the shaping of human history.

CONTENTS.

INTRODUCTION.

Chap.		Page
1.	Present State of Asia,	9
2.	Geographical Description of Asia,	13
3.	Natural History of Asia,	16
4.	Ancient and Modern Asia compared,	21
5.	General Outline of Asiatic History,	24
6.	Antediluvian age,	27

ASSYRIA.

7.	Foundation of the Kingdom of Assyria—Acbar—Nimrod—Ninus,	30
8.	Conquest of Bactria—Story of Semiramis,	32
9.	Conquests of Semiramis—Her invasion of India,	33
10.	Reign of Sardanapalus—End of the Assyrian Empire,	34
11.	The second Assyrian Empire,	36

BABYLONIA.

12.	Foundation of Babylon,	38
13.	Reign of Belshazzar—Capture and Destruction of Babylon,	40

MEDIA.

14.	Foundation of the Median Empire—Dejoces—Phraortes—Cyaxares,	42

PERSIA.

15.	Ancient Persia—Jamsheed—Zohak—Feridoon,	44
16.	Rostem—Xerxes—Gushtasp—Zoroaster,	46
17.	Alexander's Conquest—The Seleucidæ—The Sassanians—Nushirvan,	47
18.	The Mahometan Conquest of Persia—Mahmoud of Ghizni,	50
19.	Abbas the Great—Nadir Shah—Present State of Persia,	52

AFGHANISTAN AND BELOOCHISTAN.

20.	The Afghans—The Kingdom of Cabul,	54
21.	British Campaigns in Afghanistan—Manners, &c., of the Afghans,	56

CONTENTS.

THE HEBREWS OR JEWS.

Chap.		Page
22.	Origin of the Jews—Sojourn in Egypt—Conquest of Canaan,	58
23.	The Judges—The Kings—Saul—David—Solomon,	61
24.	Division of Judah and Israel—The Babylonian Captivity,	63
25.	Rebuilding of the Temple—The Maccabees,	65
26.	Jerusalem taken by Pompey—Reign of Herod—Birth of Christ,	66
27.	Rebellion of the Jews—Destruction of Jerusalem—Crusades,	68
28.	Manners and Customs of the Ancient Hebrews,	71

ARABIA.

29.	Description of Arabia—The Deserts—Yemen,	72
30.	The two races of Arabs—Their origin and character,	75
31.	Ancient Religion of the Arabs—Birth of Mahomet,	76
32.	Preaching of Mahomet—The Hejira,	78
33.	Success of Mahomet—His death,	79
34.	Progress of the Mahometans—Their mode of warfare,	80
35.	Conquest of Persia by the Saracens,	82
36.	Conquest of Syria and Egypt,	84
37.	Conquest of Spain—Decline and Fall of the Saracen Empire,	85
38.	The Wahabees,	88
39.	The Mahometan Religion,	89

PHŒNICIA.

40.	The Ancient Phœnicians—Sidon and Tyre,	92
41.	War of Nebuchadnezzar—Conquest of Tyre by Alexander,	94

SYRIA.

42.	Historical Sketch,	96

ASIA MINOR.

43.	General View of Asia Minor—Early History,	98
44.	The Kingdoms of Troy and Phrygia,	99
45.	The Kingdom of Lydia—Ionia,	100

TURKEY IN ASIA.

46.	History of the Turks,	104

ARMENIA.

47.	Historical Sketch,	107

TARTARY.

48.	Description of Tartary—The Pastoral tribes,	109
49.	The Ancient Scythians,	112
50.	Conquests of Zingis Khan,	114
51.	The Pope's Embassy to the Tartars,	115
52.	Perilous condition of the Friars in the Tartar camp,	117
53.	End of Father Ascelin's embassy,	119
54.	Adventures of Father Carpini—His description of the Tartars,	120
55.	The Tartar Dominion,	123

CHINA.

56.	Ancient History of China,	125
57.	Tartar Conquest of China,	128
58.	Conquest of China by the Mantchoos,	130
59.	Reign of Kien-Long—The Chinese Pirates,	132
60.	Recent transactions in China,	134
61.	Population, Manners, &c., of the Chinese,	136

THIBET.

Chap. | Page
62. Historical Sketch—The Grand Lama, ... 138

JAPAN.

63. Ancient History of the Japanese Empire, ... 141
64. The Portuguese and Dutch in Japan, ... 143
65. Commercial Policy of the Japanese, ... 145
66. Intercourse of the Japanese with strangers, . . 146
67. Government, Population, and Productions of Japan, . . 148

RUSSIA IN ASIA.

68. Siberia—Historical Sketch, ... 150
69. Sketches and Anecdotes of Siberia, ... 153
70. The Caucasian Countries—Colchis—Iberia—The Golden Fleece, ... 157

HINDOSTAN.

71. The Ancient Hindoos—Their Traditions, ... 161
72. Buddhism in the East—The Rajahs—Ceylon, . . . 164
73. Mahmoud of Ghizni—Aurungzebe, ... 166
74. The Portuguese in India, ... 168
75. The French in India, ... 171
76. British India, ... 172

FARTHER INDIA.

77. Description of Chin India—Burmah, ... 175
78. Cochin China—Siam, ... 178
79. Cambodia—Tonquin—Laos, ... 180

TRAVELS IN ASIA.

80. Adventures of the French Jesuits in China, . . . 182
81. Lord Macartney's Embassy to China, ... 185
82. Hardwicke's travels to the source of the Ganges, . . 189
83. The British Embassy to Persia, ... 193
84. Moorcroft's travels to Thibet, ... 196
85. Palestine—American expedition to the Dead Sea, . . 199
86. The Bedouin Arabs—The Dead Sea, ... 202

OCEANICA.

87. MALAYSIA, ... 206
88. Celebes—Its legends, ... 209
89. Borneo and the Philippines, ... 211
90. AUSTRALASIA—New Holland—Van Dieman's Land, . . 212
91. New Zealand, ... 214
92. POLYNESIA—The Society Islands—Otaheite, . . . 216
93. The Sandwich Islands—Visit of Captain Cook, . . . 220
94. Death of Captain Cook, ... 222
95. Civilization of the Sandwich Islanders, ... 224
96. Pitcairn's Island, ... 226

A PRIMARY HISTORY

OF

ASIA.

Adam naming the Animals.

INTRODUCTION.

CHAPTER I.

PRESENT STATE OF ASIA.

1. Asia is on many accounts a most interesting quarter of the globe. Here Adam and Eve were created; here was the first human family; here were the first nations; and here history itself commences.

Chapter I.—*Questions.*—1. Why is Asia interesting?

2. *History* is a record of past events. *Chronology* is a record of dates, showing when events happened. *Geography* is a description of the earth and the various countries upon it. History, therefore, includes chronology, to show when events took place, and geography, to show where they took place.

3. In the following history, we shall first give a sketch of Asia as it now is, showing its mountains and rivers, its climate, animals and vegetable products. We shall then speak of the various races of men which inhabit it, and the nations into which it is now divided.

4. It must be remembered that Asia lies to the east of America, nearly five thousand miles. The shortest way of getting to it, is to cross the Atlantic and enter the Mediterranean Sea. At the eastern end of this is Palestine, where the ancient Jews lived. This is exactly east of the United States. A person may go to Palestine in about forty or fifty days.

5. An American will find Asia very different from his own country. The people are all of very dark complexions, and many nations are nearly black. There are no rail-roads, no steamboats; instead of churches, there are mosques, pagodas and temples, where there are strange religious rites.

6. If we except a few English colonies, there are no great manufacturing establishments, no good roads, no stage-coaches, no mails, no chaises or carriages, few schools, no bibles, no improvements. Everything seems to be in a state of decay. Many places are covered over with the ruins of ancient cities. The great mass of the people are poor. Many countries once populous, are now desolate, and many once rich, are now reduced to a state of poverty.

7. In many parts, the people wander from place to place, with droves of cattle, horses and camels, and live in tents instead of houses. In some countries, the peo-

---

2. What is history? Chronology? Geography? What does history include? 3. What is to be given in this book? 4. Where is Asia? What is the shortest way to get there? Where is Palestine? How long will it take a person to go to Palestine? 5. What will an American find in Asia? 6. What of churches, roads, &c.? 7. Of the people in many countries of Asia as to their mode of living?

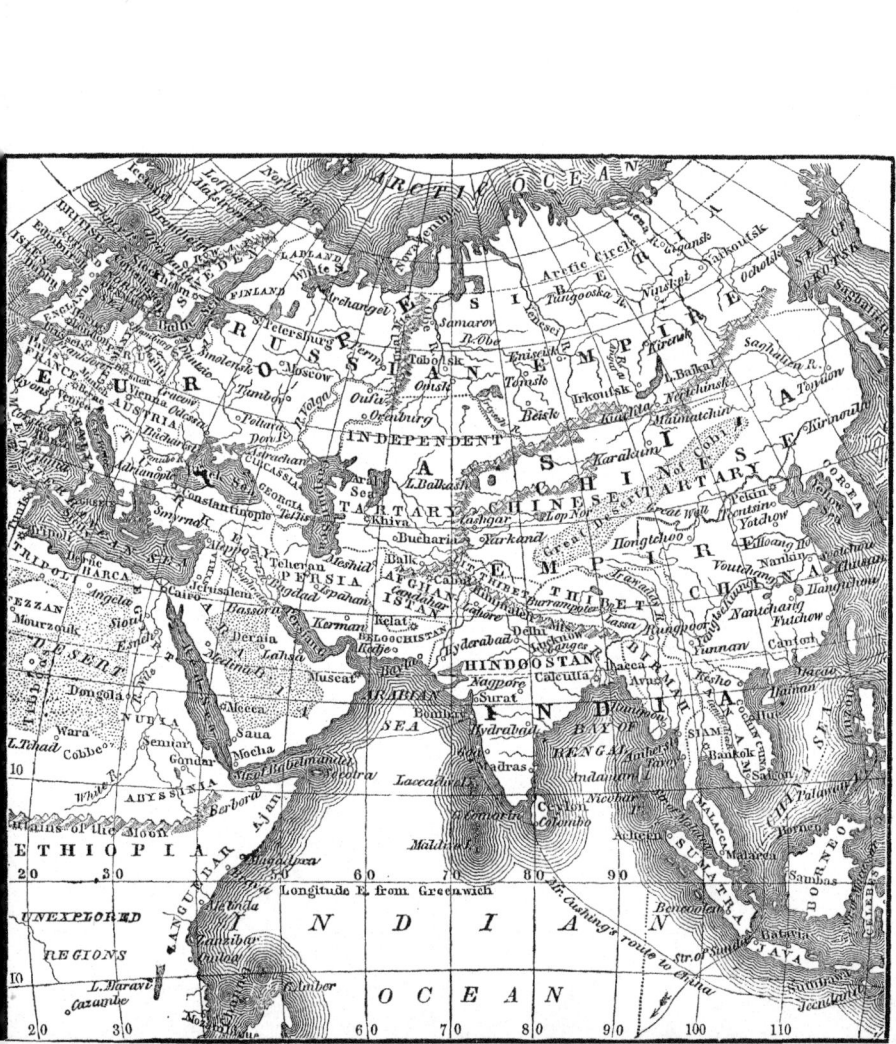

ple subsist mostly by robbery and plunder. In many parts, camels are used instead of horses, and elephants are made to carry burdens and draw loads.

8. There are, however, in Asia, many large cities; in many parts the land is very finely cultivated; in some countries, there are ingenious and useful manufactures; and there are also many valuable products, such as gems, gold, silver, indigo, silks, tea, coffee, and delicious spices.

9. Asia abounds in places of historical interest. Here are most of the places mentioned in the Bible. Here is Jerusalem, now greatly reduced; and here are the places where Babylon and Nineveh stood. Here is Mount Sinai, and Mount Lebanon, and Calvary. Here are the rivers Jordan, and Euphrates and Ganges. Here is Bethlehem, the birth-place of Jesus; and here is Mount Nebo, the tomb of Moses.

CHAPTER II.

GEOGRAPHICAL DESCRIPTION OF ASIA.

1. ASIA is the largest division of the old world. Its boundaries are chiefly formed by oceans, though it is united by land to Europe and Africa. On the north, its shores are washed by the Arctic or Frozen Ocean, which, during a great portion of the year, is covered with ice. On the east, the Pacific Ocean separates it from America. On the south lies the Indian Ocean. On the west the Red Sea and the narrow Isthmus of Suez divide it from Africa; while the Mediterranean and Black Seas and Europe, form the remainder of its western boundary.

2. In general terms, Asia may be described as 6,000 miles in length, from east to west, and 4,500 in breadth, from north to south. Its area is computed at 16,000,000 square miles.

---

8. What of cities in Asia? Manufactures? Products?
9. What of places of historical interest?
CHAPTER II.—*Questions.*—1. Describe Asia, its boundaries, &c. 2. Its size.

3. This portion of the Eastern Continent contains the loftiest mountains in the world. Indeed, the leading features of the physical geography of Asia seem to be formed on a scale of peculiar grandeur—its mountains, its table-lands, its plains, its deserts, and its rivers. The most striking object of this country, is a chain of mountains, which under various names, but with little interruption, crosses the whole continent, from the Mediterranean to the Pacific. The more remarkable portions of this range are the Taurus, the Caucasus and the Himmaleh mountains. The latter exhibit the highest points of the known world, exceeding 28,000 feet.

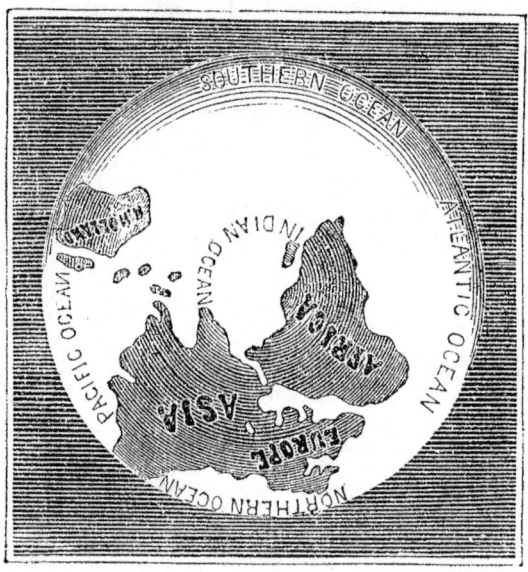

Eastern Hemisphere.

4. The Ural chain of mountains forms the boundary between Asia and Europe. The Kuen-lun or Mooz Tag, the Thian-chan and the Altaian mountains stretch east and west through the central part of the continent, and support a great extent of table-land. The chain of the Ghauts extends south only through Hindostan.

5. Asia contains a greater mass of elevated table-land than any other portion of the globe. These regions are in

---

3. Its mountains. 4. The Ural, Kuen-lun, &c. 5. Describe the steppes.

GEOGRAPHICAL DESCRIPTION OF ASIA.   15

the central part of the continent, and are called *steppes*. Many portions are mere deserts, but others are covered with rich pastures and tenanted by numerous wandering races of people, at once pastoral and warlike, whose victorious bands have often overrun and subjugated the empires of the South.

6. But the most singular feature in the form of the Asiatic continent is the depression of a considerable portion of it below the level of the ocean. The lowest part of this great basin is occupied by the Caspian Sea and the Sea of Aral. The surface of the former is 320, and that of the latter 203 feet below the level of the Black Sea, which communicates with the Mediterranean.

7. Many parts of Asia contain volcanoes, and traces of volcanic action are extended over a large portion of the interior. The Caspian Sea appears to be surrounded by a volcanic belt. The Thian-chan range exhibits many volcanic peaks, the most remarkable of which is called by the Chinese Pe-shan, or the White Mountain; it emits smoke and fire without intermission.

8. Asia has a great number of large rivers, but none of them equal in length the great rivers of America. We may distinguish in Asia three separate systems of rivers. The first comprises the most important streams of the continent. These descend from the mountain chains of the interior, and fall into the Indian Ocean, after fertilizing great tracts of country.

9. Among these are the most celebrated rivers of Asia: the Euphrates, the Indus, and the Ganges. The second class of rivers descend from the mountains which divide Tartary from Siberia, and flow north into the Arctic Ocean. The principal of these are the Obe or Obi, the Irtysch, the Yenesei and the Lena. These gloomy streams of vast length, are locked up in ice during a great part of the year, affording little aid to agriculture or the intercourse of nations.

10. The third class consists of the rivers which rise in the lofty region of the interior, and flow through China

---

6. What depressions has Asia on its surface? 7. What volcanoes? 8. What rivers? 9. Describe the most remarkable. The second class. 10. The third class.

into the Pacific Ocean, and those which course through the great plains of Western Tartary and fall into the Caspian, Aral and other inland seas. The chief of these are the Amoor, the Hoang Ho, the Yang-tse Kiang, and the Iaxartes and Oxus.

11. Asia contains several large salt-lakes, which are generally denominated *seas*. The largest is the Caspian: this is 650 miles long and 250 broad: it receives several rivers, but has no outlet. The Aral and Baikal are the next in magnitude. The Red Sea and the Persian Gulf are navigable for ships and communicate with the Indian Ocean.

12. The islands which in a geographical point of view are regarded as belonging to Asia, are numerous and important. The Japanese group lie near the eastern coast, and constitute an independent political empire. Formosa, the Loo Choo Islands and Hainan belong to China. The large and fertile island of Ceylon lies near the southern extremity of Hindostan. In the Mediterranean, near the coast of Asia Minor, are Cyprus and others famous in Grecian history. Other large islands contiguous to the south-eastern part of Asia are considered as belonging to Oceanica.

CHAPTER III.

NATURAL HISTORY OF ASIA.

1. On account of its immense extent, Asia comprises every possible variety of climate, from the dreary confines of the polar world to the heat of the tropical regions. In the south, the soil yields abundant crops of rice, which constitutes the chief food of the inhabitants of those districts. In the more temperate regions, wheat, rye and other grains are cultivated. The tea plant is a native of China, and coffee of Arabia.

2. The sugar-cane has long been cultivated in India, and the poppy-plant of that country furnishes great

---

11. What lakes and seas has Asia? 12. What islands?
CHAPTER III.—*Questions.*—1. What is said of the climate and soil of Asia? 2. Of its productions?

quantities of opium for exportation. Cotton and the mulberry grow in the southern countries, as well as various kinds of aromatic plants, including cinnamon, cassia, camphor, mace, cloves, nutmegs, &c.

Cotton Plant.

3. The Zoology of Asia is exceedingly comprehensive; yet as only a small part of the country has been scientifically explored, the subject can only be referred to here in a general manner. In the southern districts, the heat of the climate and the level nature of the country are equally favorable to a luxuriance of vegetation and the increase of animal life.

4. It is here, consequently, that we meet with numerous animals of a large size, and others of rapacious ferocity. The elephant, the tiger, the wild boar, the buffalo, the panther, the leopard, the rhinoceros, the hyena, the jackal, &c., abound in the less cultivated districts of southern Asia.

---

3. Its zoology? 4. Describe some of its animals.

5. This portion of Asia is also characterized as being the native region of those large apes which the ignorance and credulity of early travellers, led them to represent as wild men. Various species of these caricatures of the human shape are found in the great peninsulas of Hindostan, Malacca, and the adjacent islands.

Jackal.

6. In the northern parts of the continent, the zoology is much more scanty. Central Asia produces a peculiar species of Argali or sheep. The mountains of Thibet and Bootan are the native territory of a very large animal called the Tartaric ox or *Yak*. Both the camel and the horse are supposed to be originally natives of Asia. The most terrible of reptiles, the Anaconda, is found in Southern Asia: serpents of all kinds are numerous. The rivers abound with crocodiles.

7. The ornithology of Asia is very rich. This is the native country of the Peacock, the most magnificent of

---

5. Its apes. 6. Sheep, oxen, camels, reptiles, &c. 7. What of the ornithology of Asia?

NATURAL HISTORY OF ASIA.

the feathered creation; and of our domestic fowls—the most useful of breeds. Here also are produced the pheasant, the parrakeet, the parrot, &c., in great varieties. The rapacious birds are fewer than in other parts of the world.

8. Asia is chiefly inhabited by two distinct races of men, the *White*, or Caucasian; and the *Yellow*, or Mongolian. The first occupy nearly the whole western division of the continent. This race comprehends the Turks, Arabs, Koords, Persians, Afghans, Bucharians, Armenians, Georgians, Turkomans, Uzbeks, Kirghis, Hindoos, Nepalese, Cingalese, and Maldivians.

9. The second, or Yellow race, comprises the Calmucks, Khalkhas, Samoiedes, Samutes, Yonkaghirs, Tchuktchis, and Koriaks of Asiatic Russia; the Mongols, Tongouses, Mantchoos, Coreans, Japanese, Chinese, Assamites, Siamese, Birmese, and Thibetians. Besides these, we may notice two other races among the inhabitants of Asia. The Black, which appears to be a mixture of the Ethiopian, comprises but a small part of the Asiatic population, and is confined to Malacca, Ceylon, and the Andaman and Nicobar Islands.

10. The other is called the Malay race; though Malacca is its original seat, the people are now scattered over the Oceanic islands and constitute a great portion of the inhabitants.

---

8. What races of men inhabit Asia? 9. Describe their peculiarities. The Black race. 10. What of the Malays?

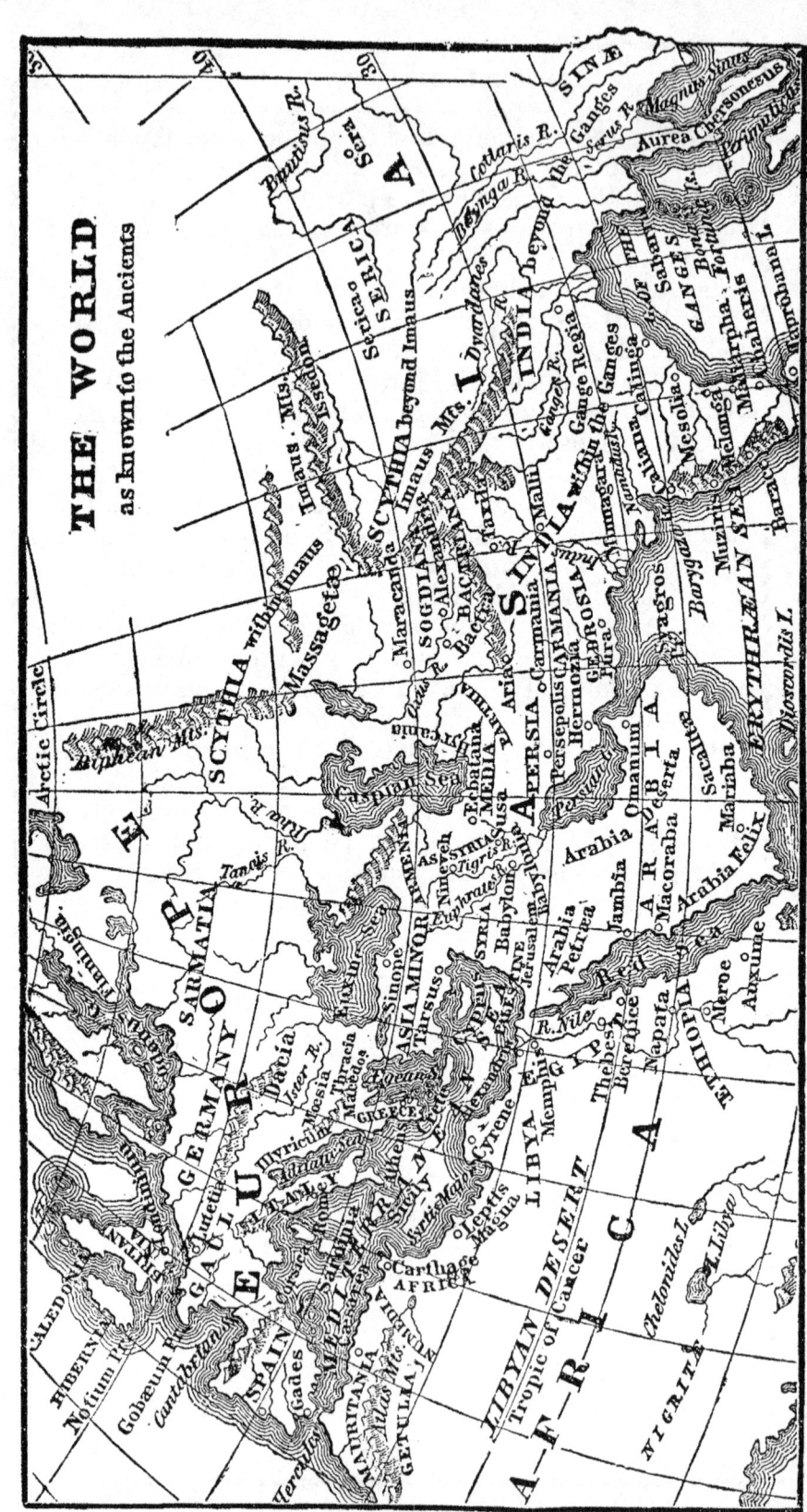

CHAPTER IV.

ANCIENT AND MODERN ASIA COMPARED.

1. Asia in ancient times was divided by geographers into the following countries: *Scythia, Sinarum Regio, India, Persia, Media, Parthia, Sarmatia, Armenia, Asia Minor, Syria, Arabia,* and *Mesopotamia.* This last included Babylonia or Chaldea.

2. The name of *Scythia* was applied to all the northern and north-eastern part of the continent. Very little was known about this region. It is comprehended in Siberia, now belonging to the Russian empire. The Sinarum Regio is supposed to have been *Cochin China.*

3. *India* was divided by the ancients into two parts, called 'India within the Ganges,' and 'India beyond the Ganges.' This country was but little known to Europe before the expedition of Alexander, 320 B. C. In

---

CHAPTER IV.—*Questions.*—1. What were the ancient divisions of Asia? 2. Where was Scythia? 3. What is said of India?

Farther India lay the *Aurea Chersonesus*, or Golden Peninsula, supposed to be *Malacca*.

4. Ancient Asia may be described in general terms as corresponding geographically to the modern country of that name, though the Persian Empire at various periods comprised other countries of vast extent. Media lay south of the Caspian Sea. Its limits varied at different times: it is now divided between Persia, Koordistan and Turkey in Asia. Under the name of Parthia were included the regions lying to the south-east of the Caspian, between Media and the river Oxus. This country now belongs to Persia and Russia.

5. Sarmatia extended from the Caucasus to an unknown extent northerly. This country is now known as a part of Siberia. Armenia still preserves its ancient name, though it is subjected partly to Turkey, and partly to Russia. Asia Minor and Syria. including Phœnicia, and Canaan or Palestine, are portions of the Turkish empire. Arabia remains, as in ancient times, independent, for the most part, of foreign dominion. Mesopotamia now constitutes a province of the Turkish dominion.

6. The institutions, the manners and customs of the people of Asia are nearly the same at the present day as they were in ancient times. No great advance has been made here for a long period, in arts, science, or learning. In disposition and temper, the inhabitants for the most part are grave, serious, and reserved. The females are generally kept in ignorance, and are not taught the art of letters. In many parts of Asia they are regarded as little better than slaves, kept in strict retirement, and do not go abroad without being veiled.

7. The Asiatic governments are generally despotic, and their administration is frequently arbitrary and tyrannical. Robbery is often practised as a regular trade, even by princes and chiefs, as an occupation held honorable and honest. Agriculture is pursued in many parts of this country, with great industry and patience, but not with the same skill as in Europe.

8. The Asiatics display great ingenuity in certain

---

4. Persia, Media, and Parthia? 5. Sarmatia, Armenia, Asia Minor, and Arabia? 6. What is said of the institutions, manners, &c., of the Asiatics? 7. Of the governments? 8. Manufactures?

manufactures, which are not surpassed for richness or beauty by those of any other part of the world. In the process of manufacturing, they employ only the most simple tools and machinery.

9. Asia has been the seat of an active and valuable commerce from the earliest known times. The internal trade is carried on chiefly by caravans, the burthens being carried by camels. The foreign commerce, particularly that of India and China, is chiefly in the hands of the English and Americans.

10. This quarter of the world has given birth to all the systems of religion now prevailing among mankind. Most of the Asiatics are Pagans, whose modes of worship embrace various forms of idolatry. Mahometanism prevails in northern Asia; Brahminism in the south, and Buddhism in the central and eastern countries. Judaism and Christianity are professed by a small number of people, chiefly in the west.

11. The following table shows the present political divisions of Asia, with the names they anciently bore.

Countries.	Square miles.	Population.	Pop. sq. m.	Religion.
Russia in Asia, or Siberia— a part of ancient Scythia.	6,100,000	6,000,000	1	Greek, Pagan, &c.
Turkey in Asia, including Asia Minor, Armenia, Syria, Phœnicia, Palestine, Assyria, Babylonia or Mesopotamia	450,000	12,000,000	27	Mahometanism.
Arabia	1,000,000	10,000,000	10	do.
Persia, including ancient Media	480,000	12,000,000	25	do.
Independent Tartary, including ancient Bactria, Parthia, &c.	700,000	7,000,000	10	do.
Afghanistan and Beloochistan, portions of ancient Persia	450,000	10,000,000	22	Mahom. & Brahmin.
Hindostan	1,000,100	130,000,000	118	Brahm. & Buddhism.
Farther India	900,000	20,000,000	22	Buddhism & Brahm.
Chinese Empire	5,400,000	280,000,000	52	Buddhism, &c.
Japan	120,000	12,000,000	100	do.

9. Commerce? 10. Religions? 11. Extent of Russia in Asia? Population? Religion?
Ask the same questions of other countries.

CHAPTER V.

GENERAL OUTLINE OF ASIATIC HISTORY.

Ruins of an Ancient City.

1. Asia has been the seat of some of the most powerful empires of ancient times, and the theatre of many of the most interesting events recorded in history. The southern part of this continent has been from the earliest ages a wealthy and populous region. Here was the cradle of civilization, and here began those great monarchies, which by absorbing into one a number of smaller original communities, have aimed so often at universal empire.

2. The political revolutions of Asia have been generally of a gigantic character. Commencing in one quarter of this continent, they have, for the most part, extended themselves in a few years to the remotest regions of Asia, and sometimes even to the centre of Europe.

3. The rapidity and facility with which political changes are accomplished in Asia, may be ascribed in some measure to the geographical nature of the country.

Chapter V.—*Questions.*—1. What is said of ancient empires? 2. Political revolutions? 3. Their causes?

GENERAL OUTLINE OF ASIATIC HISTORY.

The fertility of the soil and the warmth of the climate in some countries, have, in a manner, stifled the energies of the human mind, which require to be stimulated by wants and obstacles. This mental torpor has become hereditary in many of the Asiatic nations, and renders them the patient slaves of despotic governments.

4. In the more northern regions, races of people superior in hardihood, activity and enterprise are produced. Thus, in Asia, weak nations have been contrasted with strong ones; people, warlike, brave and active, border upon those who are effeminate, weak and timid. When wars arise in such cases, a conquest is effected with great ease and rapidity, and habits of submission and inactivity in the subjugated races, render them the unresisting slaves of their conquerors.

5. Asia was the original abode of mankind, and the seat of the first organization of society, and of the first great political empires after the antediluvian age. The Assyrian, Median, and Persian monarchies attract our notice in the first pages of Asiatic history. Hindostan and China existed as powerful and wealthy empires long before the period when those countries became known to the western nations.

6. In all the great Asiatic monarchies, cities unrivaled in wealth, splendor and population by any other region, have been built by the despots who have controlled these nations. Some of these still remain; others have fallen into decay, and their ruins now strike the eyes of the traveller with astonishment, by their extent and magnificence. Others again have totally disappeared, and the spots on which they stood cannot be identified by the geographer.

7. Oriental sovereigns still maintain the primitive custom of administering justice to their subjects in person. Though the forms of their courts and maxims of government are immutable, yet the residence of the monarch and the seat of empire are often changed. A prince on his accession to the throne, usually selects some favorite city, which is either founded by him, or

---

4. What is said of the northern regions? 5. Of the original abode of mankind? 6. Of cities? 7. Oriental sovereigns?

raised from insignificance. The monarch lavishes his wealth in embellishing the new capital, while the abodes of his ancestors are neglected. Thus Asia has been covered over with decayed cities, and the ruins of royal palaces.

8. In order to give a view of the great events of Asiatic History, we insert the following chronological table:

Before Christ, or B. C.

The creation of the world began............4004.
The Deluge took place.....................2348.
Confusion of Tongues at Babel..............2247.
Ashur founds the Assyrian empire..........2229.
Abraham goes to Canaan....................1921.
Jacob goes to Egypt.......................1705.
Moses born................................1570.
Solomon began to reign....................1015.
Persian empire established by Cyrus.......536.
Alexander invades Persia..................330.

9. Jesus Christ was born 4004 years after the creation. We mark events before Christ thus,— B. C. Events since his birth are spoken of as *in the year of our Lord*, or *Anno Domini*. We take the two first letters of these latin words, and mark modern events thus— A. D.

Anno Domini, or A. D.

Christ was crucified......................33.
Jerusalem destroyed.......................70.
Mahomet born..............................570.
Saracen empire established................638.
Japan discovered by the Europeans.........1400.
British make war on China.................1840.

10. History is divided into *Ancient* and *Modern*. Ancient history is that which treats of events before the birth of Christ. Modern history embraces events since that period.

---

8. When did the creation of the world take place? The deluge, &c.? 9. Birth of Christ? How do we mark events before Christ? Events after Christ? 10. How is history divided?

ANTEDILUVIAN AGE.

CHAPTER VI.

ANTEDILUVIAN AGE.

The Deluge.

1. THE history of mankind is made up from many sources. The Old Testament is the only book which informs us of the creation, of Adam and Eve, of their children, of the deluge, of Noah and his immediate descendants.

2. Many facts are gathered from ancient inscriptions upon temples and ruins of cities; some are collected from ancient statues, sculptures and monuments; some from old coins, medals and seals, and some from ancient manuscripts. All ancient history was originally gathered from these sources.

3. Now we have printed books, in which ancient history is collected and put in the form of connected stories

CHAPTER VI.—*Questions.*—1. How is the history of mankind made up? What of the Old Testament? 2. From what sources are many facts gathered? What of ancient history? 3. What of modern history?

or narratives. Modern history is made up from records and writings, and is not only more complete, but more clear and certain than ancient history.

4. History begins with the creation. This event occurred 4,004 years before Christ: that is, about 5,854 years ago. The whole story is told in the early chapters of Genesis. It there appears that God first created the earth, then the animals, and at last Adam and Eve.

5. These were placed in a garden, called Eden, supposed to have been situated in the valley of the river Euphrates. They disobeyed God, and were driven out of the garden, and obliged to labor for a subsistence. They had several children, among whom were Cain and Abel. These two quarrelled, and Cain slew his brother.

6. This was the first murder, the first battle—the beginning of that strife which has since cost so many lives and so much bloodshed. Cain was henceforward a miserable wanderer over the earth.

7. The family of Adam increased, and his descendants built cities and became rich. But they were also very wicked, and God sent a mighty rain, which continued for forty days, and covered the earth to the tops of the mountains with water.

8. All the people of the earth were drowned, save Noah, who had built a mighty ship or ark, in which he and his family and a vast number of animals were saved. The waters subsided at last: the ark rested on Mount Ararat, in Armenia, and Noah and his friends came forth. This age of mankind *before the flood*, is called the *antediluvian age*.

9. Noah and his children settled in the valley near the Euphrates or Tigris, and their descendants increased rapidly. Soon they were numerous, and they grew vain and proud. So they undertook to build a temple as high as the clouds, which they called Babel. But while these people were at work, their language be-

---

4. What does history begin with? How long ago did the creation take place? Where is the story of the creation told? 5, 6. Tell the story of Adam and Eve. Cain and Abel. 7. What of the family of Adam and Eve? The deluge? 8. What of Noah? What is the age before the flood called? 9. Where did Noah and his family settle?

THE TOWER OF BABEL.

came so confused that the workmen could not understand each other.

10. Smitten with dismay, the people scattered from the place. Some went one way, and settled in India and China; some settled in the north, some in the south, some in the west. Mankind from this time had a roving habit, and hence all parts of the earth became inhabited.

11. Though so many people had left the country, still many remained, and here in the country where Babel was built, certain great empires arose. The first was Assyria, and the next Babylon. Near these were the countries of Media and Persia, which also became the seats of powerful kingdoms. The history of these I shall now tell you.

---

10. Tell the story of Babel. 11. What empires arose in the region around Babel?

ASSYRIA.

CHAPTER VII.

FOUNDATION OF THE KINGDOM OF ASSYRIA—ASHUR—NIMROD—NINUS.

Semiramis in her Chariot.

1. ASSYRIA was an empire of ancient Asia, extending from Armenia on the north, to Persia on the south, and from Media on the east, to the river Tigris on the west. The exact boundaries cannot be fixed, yet the empire may, in a general view, be regarded as occupying the same territory as the modern province of Koordistan, now belonging to Turkey in Asia.

2. In ancient times, this country is said to have been remarkably fertile. Its present barrenness may be ascribed to the continual ravages of war, and the conse-

---

CHAPTER VII.—*Questions.*—1. Describe Assyria. 2. What was its ancient condition?

NIMROD—NINUS.

quent indolence and barbarism of its inhabitants. Koordistan is little better than a wilderness, inhabited by wandering tribes who live chiefly by war and plunder.

3. The great antiquity ascribed to the kingdom of Assyria, which extends far beyond the period of written records, and the fabulous spirit of the early annalists, have involved its history in great darkness. The name of this kingdom is thought to have been derived from Ashur, the second son of Shem, and the grandson of Noah. Fleeing from the tyranny of Nimrod, he came to the land of Shinar and established a settlement, which, in the course of time, became the Kingdom of Assyria.

4. This migration is supposed to have taken place soon after the dispersion of Babel. Ashur did not long enjoy his new settlement in tranquillity. Nimrod seems to have made war upon Ashur, and reduced him to subjection.

5. The sacred historian informs us that Nimrod, after having founded a kingdom in Babylonia, marched from that land into Assyria, and built Nineveh, to be the capital of that country. Ninus, his son, from whom the city was named, inherited the ambition and martial talents of his father.

6. Not satisfied with the possession of the Kingdom of Assyria, which Nimrod had bestowed upon him, he entered into a confederacy with the governor of Arabia, and at the head of their united forces, overran the Kingdom of Babylon, and put the king, with all his family, to death.

7. He then invaded Armenia, but the king of that country, by immense presents and inglorious submission, succeeded in retaining the nominal sovereignty. Ninus then turned his arms against Pharnus, king of Media, whom he conquered and afterwards put to death, with his wife and seven children. Having placed one of his dependents upon the vacant throne, he pushed his conquests still further, and during seventeen years of uninterrupted warfare, pursued his career with success.

---

3. Its antiquity and name? 4, 5. What was done by Nimrod? 6. By Ninus? 7. What of his invasion of Armenia and Media?

CHAPTER VIII.

CONQUEST OF BACTRIA—STORY OF SEMIRAMIS.

1. NINUS, returning home after these conquests, devoted himself for some time to the domestic affairs of his kingdom. He enlarged Nineveh, and adorned it with many magnificent buildings. But before long he grew weary of the inaction of a peaceful life, and again took the field against the Bactrians, whom in his previous wars he had endeavored in vain to subjugate.

2. In this campaign he is said to have marched at the head of an army comprising 1,700,000 foot, 210,000 horse, and 10,600 armed chariots. The orientals, however, have always been prone to exaggeration, and little reliance can be placed upon these extravagant numbers.

3. Ninus overran the whole of Bactria, and laid seige to the capital. His forces, however, would have been unable to subdue the strong fortifications of the city, and the martial virtue of its garrison, had not the efforts of the Assyrians been directed by the wisdom of Semiramis, a female of whose birth and education many romantic and fabulous stories are related.

4. She was the wife of Menou, one of the king's officers, and accompanied her husband in this expedition. She displayed the greatest military talent during the invasion, and the seige of the capital was conducted under her direction; the citadel was stormed, and the Bactrians were conquered.

5. Ninus, struck with admiration at her genius, took her to be his wife; for the eastern monarchs of that age had even less scruples than those of the present day in appropriating to themselves the possessions of their subjects. Semiramis bore a son to Ninus, who was called Ninyas.

6. On the death of Ninus, the young prince was left under the guardianship of Semiramis, who assumed the

---

CHAPTER VIII.—*Questions.*—1. What is said of Ninus? 2. Of the campaign of Ninus against the Bactrians? 3. Of Semiramis? 4. Her military talents? 5. Her marriage? 6. Her reign?

office of regent of the kingdom. This ambitious female employed the first years of her administration in adding to the great works and splendid monuments of the capital.

7. Palaces were built, temples were consecrated, walls were raised, lakes and canals were dug, and Nineveh was augmented, improved and embellished to such a degree that it seemed to owe its magnificence to her alone.

CHAPTER IX.

CONQUESTS OF SEMIRAMIS—HER INVASION OF INDIA.

1. SEMIRAMIS having thus raised the most splendid monuments of her power and grandeur at home, and surveyed in person all the provinces of her empire, was still unsatisfied with the measure of glory which she had acquired, and felt a desire to distinguish her reign by martial achievements.

2. She accordingly raised an immense army and first carried her conquests over a great part of Ethiopia. As the ancient writers gave the name of Ethiopians to all people of very dark complexion, we are not certain that the Ethiopia conquered by Semiramis, was in Africa.

3. Her invasion of India is narrated with more distinctness. The story is as follows: Stabrobates, the king of that country, resisted her with an army comprising a large force of elephants, which were very formidable to the invading army. Semiramis, having no elephants of her own, supplied this want by dressing up camels in such a manner as to counterfeit those animals.

4. Her arms were at first crowned with success. A fleet of war-galleys which she had built upon the Indus, obtained a victory over the Indians. The Assyrian army next overran the populous territory along the

---

Her ambition? 7. Her public works?
CHAPTER IX.—*Questions.*—1. What is said of the power and grandeur of Semiramis? 2. Of her invasion of Ethiopia? 3. Her invasion of India? 4. Her success?

banks of that river, capturing the cities and driving out the army of Stabrobates.

5. The retreat of the king, however, proved to be a stratagem. He thus decoyed the Assyrian army across the river into the heart of his kingdom. At a favorable point for his designs, he halted and faced the invaders, and a great battle ensued.

6. Semiramis placed her counterfeit elephants in the front rank of the army, and their singular appearance threw the enemy into confusion. A panic began to spread among the Indians, which would speedily have led to a general confusion and rout, had not Stabrobates made a sudden and desperate attack upon the left wing of the Assyrians, where Semiramis commanded in person.

7. He assaulted and wounded her with his own hand. She fled dismayed from the field, and her flight was the signal for the rout and dispersion of the whole Assyrian army. Thus ended the first great attempt at the invasion and conquest of India.

CHAPTER X.

REIGN OF SARDANAPALUS—END OF THE ASSYRIAN EMPIRE.

1. Semiramis having returned to her kingdom in disgrace, from her disastrous attempt to gain military glory, a plot was formed against her by her own son. This was discovered just as she was on the point of falling a victim to it.

2. Semiramis proved that she was not unworthy of a throne, by forgiving her son and resigning into his hands the sceptre which she had unjustly withheld from him. She reigned 43 years, and was succeeded by Ninyas, of whose reign nothing is related except that it was passed in indolence and inglorious ease.

5. The stratagem of Stabrobates? 6. What is said of the counterfeit elephants? 7. What was the result of the battle?

Chapter X.—*Questions.*—1. What is said of the return of Semiramis? 2. Of the end of her reign?

3. For thirty generations, the Assyrian monarchs are said to have followed the example of Ninyas, slumbering in luxury, without leaving behind them the remembrance of one action to transmit their names to posterity.

SARDANAPALUS.

4. The history of Sardanapalus, the last sovereign of this ancient empire, is more distinct. He is said to have been a prodigy of effeminate luxury, and to have adopted the dress and manners of a woman.

5. A conspiracy was formed against him by Arbaces, the governor of Media, and Belesis, the viceroy of Babylon. Sardanapalus, abandoning his life of indolence and debauchery, placed himself at the head of his army, and encountered the conspirators, whom he defeated in three pitched battles.

6. But at length the Bactrians joined in the revolt, the forces of Sardanapalus were overthrown, and the king was besieged in Nineveh. An ancient prophecy existed that the city would never be taken till the river became its enemy.

---

3. What happened in thirty generations of the Assyrian monarchy? 4. Who was the last sovereign? 5. Who conspired against him? 6. What prophecy existed at Nineveh?

7. During the siege, an inundation of the Tigris threw down a great part of the city wall. This event extinguished the last hope which Sardanapalus had cherished. He retired into the interior of his palace, where he had collected his treasures, his favorite adherents and his women.

8. Having done this, he set fire to the splendid pile, and was consumed with all its contents. The conquerors levelled the city to the ground, and put an end to the ancient empire of Assyria, about the year 876 B. C.; it having existed nearly 1400 years.

CHAPTER XI.

THE SECOND ASSYRIAN EMPIRE.

Assyrian Chariot.

1. THE history of this remote period is rather obscure, but it seems that ere long three kingdoms arose upon the ruins of the ancient Assyrian empire. One was the

---

7. What calamity happened to the city? 8. What was the end of Sardanapalus and his empire?

CHAPTER XI.—*Questions.*—1. What three kingdoms arose upon the ruins of the ancient Assyrian empire?

THE SECOND ASSYRIAN EMPIRE.

Second Assyrian Empire, of which Nineveh was the capital; one was Media, of which Arbaces became king, and the third was Babylonia, of which Belesis became king.

2. Many of the sovereigns mentioned in the Bible belonged to this second Assyrian kingdom, such as Pul, Tiglath Pileser, Sennacherib, Arphaxad, &c. It was also in the time of this kingdom that Jonah was sent to prophesy against the wickedness of the people of Nineveh.

3. In the year 606 B. C., the kings of Media and Babylon made war on Assyria. After a terrible siege, Nineveh was taken and totally destroyed. It never rose from this fatal overthrow. It had been one of the greatest cities in the world, being 50 or 60 miles in circuit.

4. Yet, in a few centuries, its ruins were buried up and its site unknown. In after times, the stones which composed its walls were dug out, and used for houses in the little city of Mosul, which stands on the side of the river Tigris opposite that where Nineveh stood.

5. A vague tradition still pointed out the place where the mighty city had been, and a few fragments of brick and stone, found in the sand, seemed to confirm this idea. A few years since, an Englishman named Layard, went thither and employed people to dig in the earth, hoping to find the ruins of the lost Nineveh.

6. Strange to tell, he succeeded in his object. Twenty feet beneath the accumulated rubbish of ages, he found the relics of superb buildings, covered with images, inscriptions and mysterious writings. Many of these curious sculptures were taken to London, and are now to be seen in the Museum there; and similar relics are also collected in the Museum of Paris.

7. From these remains, we are made to know many of the manners and customs of the Assyrians, who lived in the time of Semiramis. We here see pictures of their chariots, their dresses, their idols, their weapons, and consequently, are almost as well acquainted with their manners as if we had lived in their time.

---

2. What kings belonged to the second Assyrian empire? 3. What happened in 606 B. C.? Describe ancient Nineveh. 4. What of its ruins? What of Mosul? On what river was Nineveh situated? 5, 6. What tradition existed? What of Mr. Layard? Where are these curiosities now? 7. What do we learn from these relics?

BABYLONIA.

CHAPTER XII.

FOUNDATION OF BABYLON—DESCRIPTION OF THE CITY.

1. THE history of the city of Babylon and of Babylonia, of which it was the capital, can be traced back to a very remote antiquity. It is supposed that the kingdom was begun by Nimrod, about 2236 B. C. Babylon was probably begun on the very spot where Babel was built. It was improved and embellished by several successive kings and queens, among whom was Semiramis, who had become sovereign of the country. She is said to have made it her royal residence, and to have surrounded it with walls, nearly 2,000 years B. C.

2. This city was one of the wonders of the ancient world. It was built of a square form in the middle of a

---

CHAPTER XII.—*Questions.*—1. What is said of the antiquity of Babylon? How was it situated?

DESCRIPTION OF THE CITY.

great plain, watered by the river Euphrates. Each side of the square measured 15 miles.

3. The city, it is said, was surrounded by a wall 350 feet high, and 87 feet thick, built of large bricks cemented with bitumen, a glutinous slime which issues from the earth in that country, and which forms a most durable mortar, harder than the bricks themselves.

4. Outside the walls was a ditch, filled with water and lined with brick-work. Each side of the city had 25 gates of solid brass, and 75 towers rising over the walls, so that there were 100 gates and 300 towers, if all parts of the city had the same defences, which, however, is not altogether certain.

5. From every gate extended a straight street quite across the city, which was thus divided into exact squares. Round these squares stood the houses, which were all three or four stories in height, and built in a high style of ornamental architecture.

6. The space within the squares was vacant or occupied by court-yards and gardens. A branch of the Euphrates ran through the city from north to south, and was crossed by a bridge, at each end of which stood a magnificent palace.

7. A tunnel under the river served as an additional communication between these two palaces. The largest palace was eight miles in circuit, and contained hanging gardens, which were raised upon artificial terraces as high as the walls of the city.

8. The temple of Belus contained a lofty tower, supposed by some to be that of Babel. It was an eighth of a mile square, and 600 feet high. Here were also idols of massy gold and immense quantities of treasure. One of the statues is computed to have been worth fifteen millions of dollars.

9. Many statements given by ancient writers respecting the wonders of Babylon may have been exaggerated, but after making every reasonable abatement, there seems good ground for the belief that it was a city of extraordinary size, wealth and splendor.

---

3. What is said of its walls? 4. The ditch and gates? 5. Streets, houses, &c.? 6. Gardens, bridges, &c.? 7. Tunnel, palaces, &c.? 8. Temple of Belus? 9. Wonders of Babylon?

10. It seems to have maintained a high rank for its rich and ingenious manufactures at a very early period in the history of the world. The "goodly Babylonish garments" are mentioned in Scripture, referring to a period more than 1400 years before Christ.

CHAPTER XIII.

REIGN OF BELSHAZZAR—CAPTURE AND DESTRUCTION OF BABYLON.

1. When the Assyrian empire was overthrown, we have said that three new monarchies arose out of its ruins—Babylonia, Media and the new kingdom of Assyria. A priest and astrologer of Chaldea, named Belesis, who had assisted Arbaces in the overthrow of Sardanapalus, assumed the government of the Babylonian state.

2. He was succeeded on the throne by his son Nabonassar, and the regal dignity became hereditary in his family. Little that is remarkable occurs in the history of this monarchy for a long period of time.

3. Nebuchadnezzar II., called also Labynetus, is often mentioned in Scripture. He enlarged and embellished the capital and made war against the Jews. He captured Jerusalem and carried off the sacred utensils of the temple to Babylon.

4. Belshazzar, who reigned in the sixth century before Christ, formed an alliance with Crœsus, king of Lydia, against Cyrus, king of Persia. The confederates assembled a numerous army of Egyptians, Greeks and other people, and invaded Media, which was then governed by Darius.

5. These forces, however, were defeated by Darius, in connection with Cyrus, king of Persia. The latter marched to Babylon—another battle ensued, and the troops of Belshazzar were put to the rout. The remnant of the defeated army, with the king, fled to Babylon.

---

10. Its manufactures, &c.?
CHAPTER XIII.—*Questions.*—1. What monarchies arose out of the ruins of the Assyrian empire? 2. What is said of Nabonassar? 3. What of Nebuchadnezzar? 4. Belshazzar? 5. What of his defeat by Cyrus?

CAPTURE AND DESTRUCTION OF BABYLON.

6. The city was well furnished with provisions and the means of defence, but Cyrus laid close siege to it for two years. Finding it impossible to take the city by storm, he resorted to a stratagem.

7. Having learned that a great festival was to be celebrated in Babylon, and that it was customary with the Babylonians on that occasion, to spend the night in drunkenness and debauchery, he contrived by digging canals to turn the water of the river out of its bed, and thus, under cover of the night, marched his army through the empty channel into the city.

8. In this manner, Babylon was taken B. C. 538, and the Babylonian monarchy was overthrown. The empire of Persia now succeeded, and under Cyrus, became more powerful than Assyria or Babylonia had ever been. He did no injury to the city of Babylon, but afterwards made it his winter residence, and the third capital of his kingdom.

9. In consequence of an insurrection of the inhabitants under Darius I., who succeeded Cyrus, the walls were thrown down, and the population began to diminish. Xerxes carried away the golden statue of Belus, and Alexander the Great found the temple of that deity in ruins. Soon afterwards, Seleucus founded the city of Seleucia, in the neighborhood, and this hastened the decay of Babylon.

10. In the time of Strabo, the geographer, B. C. 30, the greater part of the city was in ruins and covered with corn-fields. At the present day, so few remains of it are discernible, that it is difficult to point out the exact spot where Babylon stood.

---

6. Of the siege of Babylon? 7. How was the city taken? 8. What was done to it by Cyrus? 9. What by Darius and Xerxes? 10. What was the condition of the city in the time of Strabo?

MEDIA.

CHAPTER XIV.

FOUNDATION OF THE MEDIAN EMPIRE—DEJOCES—PHRAORTES—CYAXARES.

1. The Medes are said to have derived their name from Madai, the third son of Japhet. They were subjugated by the Assyrian monarchs about 800 years before Christ. They remained in subjection to their conquerors till the reign of Sennacherib, when they threw off the yoke and lived for some time in a state of anarchy.

2. Their subsequent history is variously stated. It is said by some writers that the Medes at length grew weary of a life of tumult and violence, and made choice of Dejoces for their king, about 700 years B. C. This monarch built the city of Ecbatana and made it his capital.

3. He enacted various useful laws and applied himself to the civilization of the people. His mind, however, soon became engrossed with ambitious projects, and he invaded Assyria with the hope of adding it to his dominions. In this attempt he was defeated and slain, B. C. 647.

4. His son Phraortes, who succeeded him, cherished the same ambitious spirit as his father. He is said by Herodotus to have invaded and conquered Persia. It is certain that he subdued many of the surrounding nations; but having overrun a great part of Assyria, and laid siege to Nineveh, he perished, with the chief portion of his army, at that place.

5. His son Cyaxares succeeded him, B. C. 625. He also laid siege to Nineveh, but having learned that his own kingdom was threatened by an army of Scythians, he marched homeward, and was defeated in a battle with the invaders.

Chapter XIV.—*Questions.*—1. What is said of the ancient Medes? 2. Of Dejoces? 3. His laws and ambition? 4. What of Phraortes? 5. Cyaxares?

6. He attempted to retrieve his affairs, but found it impossible to prevail in arms against the brave and hardy barbarians. He therefore practised a treacherous stratagem. A truce was agreed upon, and the Scythians were invited to partake of a general feast.

7. This was served up to them by the principal families among the Medes. Each host intoxicated his guests and then massacred them. In this manner, we are told, the Medes freed themselves from their Scythian invaders.

8. The Medes then recovered the territories which they had lost, and were soon afterwards engaged in a war with the Lydians of Asia Minor. Cyaxares now entered into an alliance with Nebuchadnezzar, king of Babylon; and the two kings, joining their forces, captured Nineveh and levelled it with the ground, B. C. 606. From this overthrow, as we have before said, that great city never recovered.

9. After this victory, the Median and Babylonian empires are said to have been united; but there is great confusion in this part of ancient history; even if they were united for a time, the two monarchies appear to have existed separately at subsequent periods.

10. Cyrus, the Persian king, being now monarch of Media also, captured Babylon, as already stated, and from this time Persia became the great overshadowing empire of Asia, as we shall now proceed to show.

---

6. His stratagem? 7. How were the Medes freed from the Scythians? 8. What alliance did Cyaxares form? 9. What became of the Median and Babylonian empires?

PERSIA.

CHAPTER XV.

ANCIENT PERSIA—JAMSHEED—ZOHAK—FERIDOON.

PERSIANS.

1. Ancient Persia* comprised the territories which now constitute the kingdom of that name, although the

---

* The present kingdom of Persia is noted for the politeness and learning of its people.

The mountainous parts are occupied by robbers, who desolate the surrounding districts. In the other portions the people produce rice, wheat, cotton, tobacco, and silk, which latter is the staple of the country.

They manufacture rich carpets, shawls, tapestry, arms, porcelain, &c., but have little commerce. They have some learned men, are fond of poetry, and, on account of their politeness, are called the *French of the East*.

Chapter XV.—*Questions.*—1. Describe Ancient Persia.

ANCIENT PERSIA—JAMSHEED—ZOHAK.

ancient empire was at different times extended over many other regions. Persia, in general terms, may be regarded as extending north and south from the Caspian Sea to the Persian Gulf, and from the Jihon and Indus on the east, to the Tigris and Euphrates on the west.

2. It is very mountainous, and comprises many desert tracts interspersed with fertile valleys and plains. The deserts differ from those of Arabia in being generally salt instead of sandy. The country is for the greater part dry, having few rivers of any importance.

3. Hardly a twentieth part of the soil of Persia is under cultivation. The climate exhibits great diversities. Cyrus is represented by Xenophon as saying, "My father's empire is so large that people die of cold at one extremity and of heat at the other."

4. The Persians have many native historians, whose accounts of the early times are loaded with fables. They state that the first inhabitants of Persia lived in caves and were mere savages. Mahabad, their first king, taught them many useful arts, and began the work of civilization. He had thirteen successors, who were prophets, high priests and kings.

5. This was the golden age of Persia. The worship of fire was introduced by Hoshung, whose son Tahamurs was constantly engaged in wars with the *dives* or magicians. This prince was succeeded by Jamsheed, who founded Persepolis, and made great improvements in the social condition of the people.

6. But he soon became so tyrannical, that he was expelled from his throne by Zohak, a Syrian. The wanderings and adventures of Jamsheed, in his exile, have

---

Teheran is the capital, seventy miles from the Caspian, and is a modern city, with some fine edifices. Here the king holds his capital court, assuming the customary pomp of an Eastern sovereign. *Ispahan*, the former capital, is one of the most splendid of Asiatic cities. The royal palace is a superb structure. *Shiraz* is celebrated for its delightful climate and charming scenery.

---

2. Its mountains, deserts, &c. 3. Soil and climate. 4. What is said of the Persian historians? Who was the first king of Persia? 5. What is said of the worship of fire? Tahamurs? Jamsheed? 6. Zohak? Gao the blacksmith?

been wrought into one of the most popular romances in Persia. Zohak also proved a cruel tyrant, and was dethroned by the people, who were led on by a blacksmith of Ispahan, named Gao, or Kanah.

7. After this revolution, the blacksmith's apron became the standard of the empire, and was held in great veneration for many centuries. Feridoon, the prince who ascended the throne on the overthrow of Zohak, left this admirable lesson to his descendants: "Regard every day of your life as a page of your history: be careful, therefore, that nothing be written on it unworthy of posterity."

CHAPTER XVI.

ROSTEM—XERXES—GUSHTASP—ZOROASTER.

1. THE greatest hero of ancient Persian history is Rostem, who was a sort of oriental Hercules, and whose deeds, perhaps, are no more authentic than those of the Grecian hero. The exploits of Rostem have been magnified into miracles, and his history is consequently little better than a romance; but his name is still venerated and cherished by his countrymen with all the enthusiasm of national pride.

2. The early history of this country, as related by the native authors, differs entirely from the accounts of the Greek writers. Even the names of the kings have no resemblance. From the Greek authorities, it appears that Persia was originally a province of the Assyrian empire, and when this power was overthrown, it came under the dominion of the Medes.

3. About 600 years before Christ, Persia seems to have been an independent monarchy. Cyrus, its sovereign, conquered Crœsus, king of Lydia, and, aided by Darius the Mede, made himself master of Babylon. 536 B. C., he also became king of Media, subjugated Phœnicia, and extended his conquests over all Asia Minor. Thus he established the great Persian empire.

---

7. The blacksmith's apron? Feridoon?
CHAPTER XVI.—*Questions.*—1. Who was Rostem? 2. What is said of the native authors of Persia? 3. What of the conquests of Cyrus?

4. This famous prince is said to have lost his life in an expedition against the Scythians. 529 B. C., his son Cambyses conquered Egypt. About 500 years before Christ, the Greeks of Asia Minor revolted, and the Athenians having lent assistance to their countrymen, involved all Greece in a war with Persia.

5. An immense army was raised by Xerxes, king of Persia, for the purpose of subduing the Greeks. Five millions of men are said to have marched upon the expedition, but this is doubtless an exaggeration of the Greek historians, who are the sole authorities for the narration.

6. Xerxes crossed the Hellespont and overran nearly the whole of Greece. Athens was taken and burnt, but the Persians were defeated in a naval battle at Salamis, and compelled to withdraw into Asia.

7. During the reign of Gushtasp, a new religion was preached in Persia by Zoroaster, the Magian. He taught the worship of Fire, and made a convert of the king, who built many fire-temples, and ordered 12,000 cowhides to be finely tanned, that the precepts of the prophet might be written upon them. These were deposited in a vault at Persepolis, and priests appointed to guard them.

CHAPTER XVII.

ALEXANDER'S CONQUEST—THE SELEUCIDÆ— THE SASSANIANS—NUSHIRVAN.

1. ALEXANDER the Great, who is called in the Persian histories *Secunder Roomee*, invaded the Persian empire, B. C. 334. By the three great victories of the Granicus, the Issus and Arbela, he completely overthrew the Persian power. The unfortunate king, Darius, fleeing before the arms of the conqueror, was murdered by his own

---

4. What of Cambyses? The war of the Greeks? 5. The invasion of Xerxes? 6. What was the result of this invasion? 7. What is said of the religion of Zoroaster?

CHAPTER XVII.—*Questions.*—1. What is said of Alexander's invasion of Persia?

servants, and the whole extent of his dominions, from the Hellespont to the Indus, fell under the sway of the Macedonian warrior.

Valerian in captivity holding the stirrup for Sapor to mount his horse.

2. On the death of Alexander, Persia was assigned to Seleucus, one of his generals, who founded the dynasty of the Seleucidæ. These sovereigns reigned over the country for 62 years, when one of the tributary chiefs, named Arsaces, revolted, and established the Parthian dynasty of the Arsacidæ.

3. This was succeeded by the Sassanian dynasty, about A. D. 200. Shahpoor, or Sapor, one of the Sassanian kings, distinguished himself by his wars with the Romans. He took the emperor Valerian captive, and required him to hold his stirrup when he mounted his horse.

4. During his reign, Mani, the founder of the religious sect of the Manichæans, began to propagate his opinions. He attempted to combine Christianity with the doctrine of Zoroaster; but he was put to death by order

---

2. What became of Persia after the death of Alexander? What is said of Arsaces? 3. Of the Sassanians and Shahpoor? 4. Of Mani and his religion?

of the king, and his skin was stripped off and hung up at one of the gates of the capital.

5. The Sassanian dynasty gained its greatest glory in the reign of Khosrou Nushirvan, who succeeded to the throne, A. D. 513. This prince was distinguished by his great talents and humane disposition, and he is esteemed by the oriental historians as the most illustrious monarch that ever reigned in Persia.

6. Nushirvan reformed abuses in the government, fixed the revenue system, founded schools and colleges, and gave encouragement to learned men of every country who resorted to his court. The celebrated fables of Pilpay were procured by his order from Hindostan, and translated into Persian.

7. He also caused to be written a moral work, entitled "*Instructions for all Degrees of Men*," and gave a copy to every family in his empire. No monarch was ever more zealous in promoting the happiness of his people than Nushirvan. His impartial administration of justice, and his vigilance in detecting and punishing every act of oppression in his inferior officers, gave confidence and security to all his subjects.

8. Many anecdotes are recorded of his rigid equity, which seems to have been a prominent feature in his character. He was named by the Arabs Al Malek, or the Just, and Mahomet was accustomed to boast of his own good fortune in having been born in the reign of so worthy a sovereign.

9. A Roman ambassador, one day, admiring the prospect from the windows of Nushirvan's palace, observed an uneven piece of ground, and inquired why it was not made uniform with the rest. He was told that it was the property of a poor woman who refused to sell it, and that the king chose to have his prospect spoiled rather than commit injustice by seizing it. The Roman replied, "That irregular spot appears more beautiful than all the surrounding landscape, for it is consecrated to justice."

---

5. Of Khosrou Nushirvan? 6, 7. What was the character of his government? 8. His equity? 9. What anecdote is related of a Roman ambassador?

CHAPTER XVIII.

THE MAHOMETAN CONQUEST OF PERSIA— MAHMOUD OF GHIZNI.

Firdusi writing the Shah Nameh.

1. The Khalif Omar, who succeeded Mahomet, carried his arms into Persia, and after a long struggle, the Arabs were victorious. Yezdijird, the Persian king, was driven from his throne A.D. 638, the Mussulman armies spread themselves over the country, destroying with fanatic fury every vestige of the ancient Persian religion, and the inhabitants were compelled to adopt the creed of the conquerors or seek an asylum in other lands.

2. Persia thus became a Mahometan country and continues so to this day. The country, however, was only a province of the empire of the Khalifs of Bagdad, and followed the many revolutions to which that power was subjected.

Chapter XVIII.—*Questions.*—1. What is said of Khalif Omar and Yezdijird? 2. What became of Persia after the conquest?

3. While the kingdom was thus divided and distracted by the dissensions of its rulers, the standard of independence was raised by Yakoob ben Leis, the son of a pewterer and himself a robber. He was a person of great courage and enterprise, and having gathered around him a band of devoted adherents, he made war upon the Khalif, rescued nearly all Persia from his dominion, and fixed the seat of the new government at Shiraz, A. D. 877.

4. Mahmoud, of Ghizni, a city in what is now called Afghanistan, was one of the greatest and most successful monarchs of the east. From being the chief of a petty principality, he rose to be the Sultan of Persia, and carried his victorious arms over the neighboring territories, from Georgia to the Indian Ocean, A. D. 1010.

5. Mahmoud was renowned not only for his victories, but for the patronage which he bestowed upon men of genius. It is to his love of literature that the Persians are indebted for the noble work of the poet Firdusi, entitled *Shah Nameh*, or the Book of Kings, a splendid epic or narrative poem which contains the substance of all the ancient Persian history.

6 The conquests of Mahmoud in the east were uniformly marked by religious persecution, and his bigoted Mahometan zeal led him not only to destroy the idols of Hindostan, and pillage the temples of the idolaters, but also to destroy the cities and cover the land with desolation.

7. In a popular eastern tale, the vizier of this prince is represented as pretending to be acquainted with the language of birds. Seeing, one day, two owls perched together, apparently in conversation, he told the Sultan that the old owl was offering a hundred ruined villages as a dowry to her daughter, who was about to be married, and that she concluded by exclaiming, "Heaven grant a long life to Sultan Mahmoud, and we shall never want for ruined villages!"

---

3. Who was Yakoob ben Leis? 4. Mahmoud of Ghizni? 5. The Shah Nameh? 6. What was the character of the conquests of Mahmoud? 7. What story is related of him?

CHAPTER XIX.

ABBAS THE GREAT—NADIR SHAH—PRESENT STATE OF PERSIA.

The poet Hafiz.

1. The glories of Mahmoud soon passed away, and Persia was overrun by successive invasions of the Tartars and Turks. The country during many centuries became a dreadful theatre of war and devastation. It was at this period, however, that Hafiz,* the greatest of Persian poets, flourished. The people possessed a native energy, by which they ultimately

---

* Hafiz was a native of Shiraz, and died about 1389. In his time, Persia was subject to the sultan of Bagdad, who invited him to his court. He is said to have had an interview with Tamerlane, who conquered Shiraz in 1387. His poems are chiefly devoted to the celebration of love and wine; many of them are committed to memory by the people of Persia, and often sung and recited.

Chapter XIX.—*Questions.*—1. By what nations was Persia overrun? What of the poet Hafiz?

ABBAS THE GREAT—NADIR SHAH.

succeeded in throwing off the yoke of their conquerors and oppressors.

2. In the beginning of the 16th century, Abbas, surnamed the Great, ascended the throne. He governed with strict justice, and by encouraging every species of industry, restored the country to a high state of prosperity.

3. After flourishing for more than two centuries, Persia was desolated in the most cruel manner by the successful invasion of the Afghans in 1722, who carried fire and sword throughout the kingdom, and reduced the fairest cities to ashes.

4. Kouli Khan, who was originally a leader of banditti, turned his arms against the invaders, expelled them from the country, and ascended the throne in 1736, with the title of Nadir Shah. This monarch afterwards invaded the Mogul empire of Hindostan, where he obtained an enormous treasure in gold and jewels.

5. But the death of Nadir, without leaving any regular successor to the crown, caused a long and furious civil war which rent the kingdom in pieces. At length, Kureem Khan, one of Nadir's officers, obtained the sovereignty, and during a reign of sixteen years, endeavored to heal the wounds of the country. His death in 1779 led to new civil wars.

6. Futeh Ali Shah, who came to the throne in 1796, reigned in comparative tranquillity, although he was unfortunate in his wars with Russia, by which he lost some of his northern territories. Shah Mohammed, his grandson, ascended the throne in 1834, and reigned till 1848, when he was succeeded by the present reigning sovereign, Nessur ud Doon Shah.

7. The government of Persia is an unrestricted despotism; the sword is the only authority. A most unfortunate circumstance in the condition of Persia is the number of hordes of banditti by which the country is ravaged. Even those who defend the land in war, plunder it in peace.

---

2. What is said of Abbas the Great? 3. Of the Afghans? 4. Who was Kouli Khan? 5. What happened after his death? 6. Who was Futeh Ali Shah? Who was Shah Mohammed? 7. What is the government of Persia?

8. These predatory bands lurk among the mountains and deserts in every part of the kingdom, from which they issue forth in great numbers to plunder the cultivated plains and attack the caravans of travellers. In consequence of this, many of the finest tracts are now abandoned by the husbandman and given up to these marauders.

9. The suppression of this system of robbery was one of the grand objects of the policy of Abbas, which he pursued by vigorous measures. The present monarch, less energetic, seems to have taken no determined step to accomplish this salutary purpose.

AFGHANISTAN AND BELOOCHISTAN.

CHAPTER XX.

THE AFGHANS—THE KINGDOM OF CABUL.

1. The country of the Afghans* is sometimes called Independent Persia, and sometimes the Kingdom of Cabul. It lies between Persia Proper and Hindostan. This country was very little known or regarded by the ancients, who called it *Arachosia* and *Paropamisus*. Alexander, on his route to India, was obliged to penetrate through the defiles of Cabul where he encountered formidable obstacles.

---

* Afghanistan and Beloochistan, lying between Persia and Hindostan, are occupied by warlike and enterprising tribes.

The Afghans are a bold, vigorous race, who have made considerable advances in civilization. They are of simple manners, and great hospitality. Schools are said to exist in every village. *Cabul*, the capital, is delightfully situated on a branch of the Indus. *Peshawur*, *Candahar*, and *Ghizni*, are large and important towns.

The *Belooches* are the leading tribe in *Beloochistan*. They are fierce and warlike, and addicted to plunder. *Kelat* is the residence of the khan or chief.

8, 9. What is the condition of the country?
Chapter XX.—*Questions.*—1. What is said of the country of the Afghans? What of Alexander?

2. In fact, the inaccessible nature of a great part of this country, the poverty of the inhabitants, and the fierceness of their disposition, have all contributed to deter foreign invaders from designs of conquest here, and thus have secured the independence of the Afghans.

3. For a long series of years, these people, safe among their mountain recesses, retained their early customs and original character. All that the rest of the world knew of them was, that they were conspicuous for their warlike and restless disposition.

4. In the 11th century, the city of Cabul was in the possession of Mahmoud, of Ghizni, and was at that time an important place. But his dynasty was crushed by the invasion of the Tartar leaders, Zingis Khan and Timour, and Cabul became united to Hindostan under the Mogul empire.

5. When that empire was dismembered, the hardy population of Cabul re-asserted their independence, and in the early part of the 18th century they invaded Persia and made themselves masters of the whole kingdom. Their dominion was exercised with the most sanguinary severity, and Persia was rendered almost desolate.

6. At length, Nadir Shah, as we have just related, put himself at the head of his countrymen and expelled the Afghans with great slaughter. He also established his own authority in Afghanistan; but at his death, the independence of the country was again restored by Ahmed Shah, an Afghan chief, who afterwards became its sovereign, with the title of King of Cabul.

7. Ahmed then invaded Hindostan, where he broke the power of the Mahrattas, who were about to seize the fallen sceptre of the Great Mogul. His success enabled him to extend his dominion over some of the finest provinces of India, and the kingdom of Cabul thus became one of the most powerful monarchies in Asia.

8. After the death of Ahmed, however, this kingdom was broken up by dissensions among his family, and the

---

2. What is the nature of the country? 3. What is the early history of the people? 4. What is said of the city of Cabul? 5. What of the Afghan invasion of Persia? 6. Of Nadir Shah? 7. Of Ahmed and his successors? 8. What happened after the death of Ahmed?

Afghan power was restricted within the limits of their native territory.

9. Beloochistan was called Gedrosia by the ancients. At one time, it was considered a part of Persia, and in later times, a part of Afghanistan. Alexander lost a considerable part of his army in crossing a desert here. No event of interest has occurred in modern times within this territory. Indeed, the state of the nation is imperfectly known; it can hardly be considered as within the pale of civilization.

CHAPTER XXI.

BRITISH CAMPAIGNS IN AFGHANISTAN—MANNERS, ETC., OF THE AFGHANS.

1. THE British in India became involved in a war with the Afghans in 1838. They invaded Cabul with a strong army, deposed the reigning sovereign, and placed on the throne Shah Soojah, who had formerly held possession of it, but was expelled by a revolution.

2. British garrisons were established in the country to maintain the authority of the sovereign, and the inhabitants remained in quiet subjection till 1841, when they rose in insurrection, put the British commander to death, and drove the troops out of the country with great slaughter.

3. During the following year, the British returned to Cabul with a powerful force, and destroyed the greater part of the city. They also devastated the country and burnt many towns; but the Afghans preserved their independence, and have continued to maintain it to the present day.

4. The Afghan monarchy is remarkably distinguished from all other Asiatic governments. Instead of being an arbitrary despotism, it has a large infusion of the popular element. There is a representative assembly

---

9. What of Beloochistan? Its history?

CHAPTER XXI.—*Questions.*—1. What is said of the British invasion of Afghanistan? 2. When did the Afghans revolt? 3. What was the conduct of the British in this country? 4. What is the character of the Afghan monarchy?

in every tribe, without whose consent the sovereign can do nothing.

5. The Afghans are a very superior people, considered as Asiatics. Their martial and lofty spirit, their bold and simple manners, their sobriety and contempt of pleasure, their unbounded hospitality, and the general energy and independence of their character, place them in a strong and striking contrast to the timid and effeminate Hindoos, on whom they immediately border. Among the Hindoos, every movement originates with the government or its agents, and the people are accounted as nothing.

6. The established religion in Afghanistan is Mahometanism, though the people are remarkably tolerant. A taste for knowledge is general among them. The country is divided like the ancient kingdom of Israel, according to the tribes which inhabit it. The Ensofzies, who occupy the north-eastern corner of this region, exhibit the most complete specimen of the original Afghan rudeness.

7. These are the most independent of the whole race of Afghans, and scarcely own any subordination whatever. The mountaineers, in particular, are excessively rude and ignorant. One of them seeing a Mollah or religious doctor copying the Koran, drew his sword and struck off his head, exclaiming, "You tell us this is the book of God, and yet you make it yourself!"

---

5. What of the people? 6. Of their religion? 7. Of the Ensofzies?

THE HEBREWS OR JEWS.

CHAPTER XXII.

ORIGIN OF THE JEWS—SOJOURN IN EGYPT—CONQUEST OF CANAAN.

Joseph is sold in Egypt to an Officer of Pharaoh's Household.

1. PALESTINE,* or the Holy Land, which was the seat of the Hebrew commonwealth, and subsequently of the kingdoms of Israel and Judah, lies at the eastern

---

* *Palestine* was called *Canaan*, or the *Land of Promise* by the Jews. The name Palestine is derived from the Philistines, who anciently inhabited a part of it. This country is now regarded as a part of Syria, and is under the government of Turkey. The people of the country are chiefly Turks, Arabs, and mixed races; but few Jews inhabit it. Jerusalem is reduced to an inferior town, with 15 or 20 thousand inhabitants. The remains of many places mentioned in the New Testament are still visible. The chief river is the Jordan, which flows through the lake or sea of Galilee, and empties into the Dead Sea. Pa-

---

CHAPTER XXII.—*Questions.*—1. Describe Palestine.

extremity of the Mediterranean, between Phœnicia on the north, and Idumea on the south: the Dead Sea, or Lake Asphaltites, the river Jordan, and the Sea of Galilee bounded it on the east.

2. It is a mountainous country, with a great diversity of soil and climate. At present, it exhibits a general aspect of barrenness and desolation; but were the country under a good government, it might be rendered, by means of industry, one of the fairest parts of the earth.

3. The Hebrews, Israelites, or Jews, are the descendants of the patriarchs Abraham, Isaac and Jacob. Abraham was born at Ur, of the Chaldees, a town in Padan-Aran or Mesopotamia, about 2000 years B. C., and was descended, in the eighth generation, from Shem, the second son of Noah.

Abraham sending away Hagar and Ishmael.

4. Abraham resided in Palestine, then called *Canaan*, where he became rich in gold, silver and cattle, and had

---

lestine is poorly cultivated, and far less populous than in ancient days. In the time of Christ it contained some millions of inhabitants.

---

2. Its present condition. 3. From whom are the Hebrews descended? 4. What is said of Abraham?

a numerous household. He had two sons—Isaac, the progenitor of the Hebrews, and Ishmael, who, with his mother Hagar, was sent away by Abraham, and came near perishing in the wilderness. The affecting story is told in Genesis, chapter 16-21. Isaac remained in Canaan.

5. Esau, the eldest son of Isaac, settled in Edom, on the borders of Canaan, and was the ancestor of the Edomites. Jacob, the younger son, whose name was afterwards changed to *Israel*, was the father of twelve sons, from whom the twelve tribes of Israel descended. Joseph, one of these twelve, was sold by his brethren as a slave to some Arabian merchants, by whom he was carried into Egypt.

6. There he became the chief minister of Pharaoh, the king. His brethren having come into that country to purchase corn, he made himself known to them, and persuaded them and his father to settle in Egypt, where the rich territory of Goshen was assigned to them for a residence.

7. In process of time, the Israelites became so numerous in Egypt, that they excited the alarm of the Egyptians. Being ill-treated, they departed from the country. B. C. 1491. Under the guidance of Moses, and aided by a series of miracles from heaven, they reached the borders of the land of Canaan, which had been promised to them for a perpetual possession.

8. Here Moses died, after framing a code of laws, by divine direction, for the political and religious government of the nation. The Israelites crossed the Jordan and invaded Canaan. After a long struggle, they made themselves masters of the country, and established themselves, permanently, there.

Ishmael and Hagar? 5. Esau, Jacob, and Joseph? 6. Joseph's brethren? 7. Of the Israelites in Egypt? 8. Of Moses and the conquest of Canaan?

CHAPTER XXIII.

THE JUDGES — THE KINGS — SAUL — DAVID — SOLOMON.

King David.

1. On the first establishment of the Israelites in the conquered territory, they formed twelve separate republics, of the twelve tribes, each having specific bounds, and each preserving its own chiefs and elders. The worship of Jehovah, however, formed a common bond of union, which united them into one federal state.

2. The national affairs were administered by magistrates, with the title of *Shophetim*, called *judges* in Scripture. From the days of Joshua, under whom the conquest of Canaan was effected, to the time of Saul, the first king, about three centuries and a half elapsed. This period has been called the *heroic* age of Israel.

CHAPTER XXIII.—*Questions.*—1. What was the early government of the Israelites? 2. How were their national affairs administered?

3. Every man, during this period did what seemed good in his own eyes, and the nation acknowledged no sovereign but Jehovah. Personal courage and military talents were the qualities most esteemed in a ruler, and the judges were the leaders of armies, rather than the expounders of law.

4. Of these individuals, the most renowned were Othniel, Gideon, Jephthah, Samson and Samuel. Samson was noted for his prodigious strength; nearly all his recorded feats are miraculous or superhuman. He is believed, by some, to be the original of the Hercules of the Greeks and other heathen nations.

5. Samuel was the last of the judges, and was also a prophet. He purified the religious worship, reformed the manners of the nation, and drove out the Philistines. His last act of authority, and which he performed with reluctance, but at the earnest wish of the people, was the anointing and crowning Saul as king, B. C. 1095—thus changing the government from a republic to a monarchy.

6. David obtained the daughter of Saul in marriage, and after a long series of adventures, succeeded to the crown on the death of his father-in-law, B. C. 1056. He overthrew the Philistines, Moabites and Amalekites, all of whom bordered on Canaan; he also took Jerusalem and made it his capital.

7. David compelled the Syrians and Edomites to become tributary to Israel. He conquered all the land from the mountainous country near the sources of the Euphrates to the borders of Egypt. But though a great warrior and statesman, David is still more celebrated for his sacred hymns, which appear in the Bible under the name of *Psalms*. Solomon succeeded his father David, B. C. 1015, and married the daughter of the king of Egypt.

8. The reign of Solomon was the golden age of Israel. The proofs which he gave of wisdom and discernment were so celebrated throughout the East, that the most powerful monarchs entered into alliance with him. His name is still proverbial in that quarter of the world for wisdom, learning and magnificence.

---

3. What is said of the time of the Judges? 4. Who were the most famous? 5. What is said of Samuel? 6. David? 7. Solomon? 8. His reign?

9. Solomon built a splendid temple at Jerusalem, which he dedicated, at a solemn festival, to the worship of Jehovah. He opened a trade with Egypt and the countries south of the Red Sea. He also built or enlarged the city of Tadmor, in the Syrian desert, which afterwards became famous under the name of Palmyra.

CHAPTER XXIV.

DIVISION OF JUDAH AND ISRAEL—THE BABYLONISH CAPTIVITY.

Jews in captivity: a prophet reading and explaining to them the promises of the Covenant.

1. Toward the close of the reign of Solomon, the kingdom of Israel declined in power and prosperity. The people were oppressed with a heavy burden of

---

9. What is said of the temple? Tadmor?
Chapter XXIV.—*Questions.*—1. What is said of the decline of the kingdom of Israel?

taxation; the purity of religious worship declined, and the idolatries of foreign nations began to be adopted.

2. On the death of Solomon, B. C. 975, his son Rehoboam succeeded him. By his haughty and arrogant behavior toward the northern tribes, he so far alienated their affection, that they rebelled against his authority and set up Jeroboam as a rival king.

3. Thus the nation became divided into two kingdoms, *Israel* and *Judah*. The former comprised the ten northern tribes, and the latter those of Judah and Benjamin. Israel was the larger and more populous, but Judah was the more wealthy kingdom, and retained possession of the chief city and national temple as well as of the established priesthood.

4. By this fatal schism in the Hebrew nation, its power received a blow from which it never recovered. Obstinate and bloody wars arose between the two kingdoms; both were weakened, and thus gradually became a prey to their heathen enemies.

5. Idolatry made its way both in Israel and Judah. The latter was soon punished by an invasion of the Egyptians, who, under Shishak, their king, captured Jerusalem, B. C. 971, and stripped the temple of Solomon of all the wealth which had been amassed there during the long and peaceable reign of its founder.

6. The kingdom of Israel survived the division of the original monarchy 253 years. During this period the people gradually lost all the purity of their ancient religious worship, and became worshippers of idols.

7. At length, Shalmaneser, king of Assyria, made war against Israel, took Samaria, the capital, and led the inhabitants away captive, B. C. 729. This event is called the captivity of the ten tribes. The captives were transported into some distant region beyond the Euphrates, and the kingdom of Israel was divided among a body of Assyrian colonists.

8. The kingdom of Judah lasted about a century and a half longer, under the dynasty of the house of David,

---

2. Of Rehoboam? 3. The division of the kingdom? 4. What was the consequence of this? 5. What is said of idolatry? Of the capture of Jerusalem? 6. Of the kingdom of Israel? 7. Of the captivity of the ten tribes? 8. What was the end of the kingdom of Judah?

till at length Nebuchadnezzar, king of Babylon, after repeated invasions, captured Jerusalem, demolished the temple, and carried the Jews away captive to Babylon, B. C. 588.

CHAPTER XXV.

REBUILDING OF THE TEMPLE—THE MACCABEES.

1. The ten tribes of Israel who were carried beyond the Euphrates never returned. All traces of them in history have been lost, and various ingenious conjectures have been formed as to what became of them. It has even been suggested that the American Indians are their descendants, but of this there is not the slightest evidence.

2. The character of the Jews suffered a considerable change during the Babylonish captivity. They became more exclusively attached to their country and their ancient laws. They strictly avoided intermarriage with foreigners, and gradually adopted that unsocial spirit towards all men, except their own nation, for which they have been so often reproached.

3. Misfortune had soured their temper, while the expectation of a Messiah or anointed King, who had been announced by their prophets, kept alive the national pride. After 70 years' captivity, Cyrus king of Persia, who had overthrown the Babylonish monarchy, set the Jews at liberty and permitted them to return to the land of their forefathers, and rebuild the temple and city of Jerusalem.

4. They accordingly assembled under Zerubbabel, a descendant of their ancient kings. After many obstacles and delays, the *second temple* as it is called, was finished and dedicated B. C. 515.

CHAPTER XXV.—*Questions*.—1. What is said of the lost tribes? 2. Of the character of the Jews? 3. Of their misfortunes? Of the Messiah? 4. Of their return to Jerusalem?

5. The Assyrian settlers in Samaria and a small remnant of the Hebrews, who had remained in the land after the conquest, formed another nation called *Samaritans*. These retained a corrupt form of the ancient Mosaic worship. Between the Jews and the Samaritans a bitter and irreconcilable hatred always existed.

6. From the period of the restoration, the Jewish nation continued for three centuries and a half to be tributary in succession to the Persians, Greeks, Egyptians and Syrians. Under these different masters the local government was frequently administered by Jewish high priests, yet the people were often grievously oppressed.

7. At length the Jews rose against the Syrians, and chose Judas Maccabæus for their leader, B. C. 163. They defeated them in various battles and regained their independence. The high priests were now the chief magistrates of the nation: but before long, Aristobulus, a descendant of Judas Maccabæus assumed the crown as king of the Jews.

8. The descendants of Aristobulus were called *Asmoneans*. The sects of the Pharisees and Sadducees now began to distract the nation with their factious contentions, and soon plunged it into a civil war. One party called in the king of Arabia to their assistance; the others sought the aid of the Romans, and by their help drove the Arabians out of the country.

CHAPTER XXVI.

JERUSALEM TAKEN BY POMPEY—REIGN OF HEROD—BIRTH OF CHRIST.

1. At this period Pompey the Great was commander-in-chief of the Roman armies in the East. The Jews agreed to make him the umpire in their dispute. Pompey gave his decision, but the party which esteemed it-

---

5. Of the Samaritans? 6. What were the fortunes of the Jewish nation? 7. Their insurrections? 8. Of the Asmoneans, Pharisees, &c.?
CHAPTER XXVI.—*Questions.*—1. What is said of Pompey?

self the least favored in this judgment, instead of acquiescing, took up arms against the Romans.

2. Pompey immediately marched against Jerusalem. The Jews were still so scrupulous with regard to their religion, that they would do nothing on the Sabbath to prevent the besiegers from carrying on their works. By taking advantage of this, the city was captured by the Romans, B. C. 63.

Christ sending forth his disciples.

3. The walls of Jerusalem were demolished and a Roman garrison was placed in the citadel. Yet under the Roman dominion, the Jews were constantly engaged in factions and wars with each other. Jerusalem was also pillaged by Crassus, the Roman triumvir, on his expedition against the Parthians. He took from the temple all the money of the treasury and the sacred utensils, amounting in value to ten millions of dollars.

4. After the death of Pompey, Julius Cæsar visited Judea and granted liberty to the Jews to fortify Jerusalem and rebuild the walls. Herod, an Idumean, was

---

2. His attack on Jerusalem? 3. How were the Jews treated by the Romans? 4. By Julius Cæsar?

now placed on the throne, but subject to the Roman government.

5. Herod was one of the greatest tyrants known in history: he manifested a thorough contempt for the Jewish religion, and introduced heathenish customs which made him still more odious to his subjects. Notwithstanding this, he adorned Jerusalem with stately buildings, among which was a third temple, built in a style of magnificence superior to that of Solomon.

6. During the reign of Herod, OUR SAVIOUR was born at Bethlehem in Judea. After the death of Herod, procurators or governors were appointed instead of a king. One of these was Pontius Pilate, under whose administration Jesus Christ was put to death. Having risen from the dead he sent his disciples forth, who extended the gospel in various countries.

7. Agrippa, the grandson of Herod, was afterwards made king of Judea, but on his death the administration by governors was renewed. These petty tyrants so oppressed the people that great numbers of them abandoned their country and never returned.

CHAPTER XXVII.

REBELLION OF THE JEWS—DESTRUCTION OF JERUSALEM—CRUSADES.

1. AT length in the year 67 A. D., the Jews rose in rebellion against the Romans. An army under Vespasian was sent against them: his success was great and rapid, for the Jews instead of uniting to oppose him and save their country, were split into factions animated with the most bitter hatred of each other.

2. These obstinate and infatuated people had long meditated a resistance to the Roman power, hoping to find protection from Heaven which their impieties had deeply offended. Their own historian represents them

---

5. What is said of Herod? 6. Of the birth of our Saviour and his death? 7. Of Agrippa?

CHAPTER XXVII.—*Questions.*—1. When did the Jews rebel against the Romans? 2. What were their expectations?

as having reached the highest pitch of iniquity, while famines, earthquakes and prodigies all combined to forebode their approaching ruin.

3. Their dissensions were not confined to Jerusalem, but spread through all the villages, towns and cities of Judea. Even houses and families were divided against each other. But Jerusalem was the chief theatre of their contentions, and was stained with civil bloodshed and butcheries of the most horrid description.

4. The command of the Roman army was now assumed by Titus the son of Vespasian, and he advanced to besiege Jerusalem, A. D. 72. This for a short time suspended the intestine discords of the Jews, but they quickly burst out again with greater fury than ever.

5. Titus wished, if possible, to preserve the city, and made pacific overtures to the inhabitants, but these were rejected. The Jews deceived by false prophets, who promised a deliverance, persevered in their hostility long after every reasonable chance of success had disappeared.

6. They fought against each other in the streets of Jerusalem, while the walls of the city shook under the battering-rams of the Romans, and they refused the proffered mercy of Titus when his victorious standards were planted on the battlements.

7. Dreadful was the punishment of this ill-fated nation: their city and temple were reduced to heaps of shapeless ruins, and the best and bravest of the people fell by the swords of the Romans or of each other. The destruction of Jerusalem was accomplished, and the greater part of the inhabitants of Judea were dispersed over the earth to become a mockery, a by-word and a reproach among nations.

8. In more modern times, Palestine has been the theatre of interesting events. In the seventh century, it was conquered by the Saracens, and afterwards by the Turks. In the middle ages it became the fashion with religious people to make pilgrimages to Jerusalem. The pilgrims being harshly treated by the Turks, a

---

3. Their dissensions? 4, 5. What is said of Titus? 6. What was the behavior of the Jews? 7. How were they punished? 8. What of the Saracens? Pilgrims? Crusades?

frenzy seized the warriors and fanatics of Europe, and in the eleventh century, several crusades were made for the purpose of capturing the holy city.

Crusaders in sight of Jerusalem.

9. The crusades consisted of armies, in some instances very numerous and led by celebrated knights and princes. They succeeded in capturing Jerusalem, A. D. 1099, and held it for 150 years, when it was conquered by the celebrated Saladin, a Mahometan chief, who then ruled over Egypt.

10. The Jews are to be found in all the great cities of Europe, and are supposed to number three millions at the present day. They rarely marry with other people. They preserve their ancient worship, and expect at some future day to be restored to their country and to prosperity.

---

9. What of Jerusalem? Saladin? 10. What of the Jews at the present day?

CHAPTER XXVIII.

MANNERS AND CUSTOMS OF THE ANCIENT HEBREWS.

1. The course of domestic life among the ancient Hebrews was simple and uniform to a remarkable degree. They had nothing of that variety of studies and pursuits, that multiplicity of arts, conditions and employments which existed among many other ancient nations.

2. All the people enjoyed the same equal liberty. All of them, as being the offspring of the same ancient stock, boasted an equality of lineage and rank. There were no empty titles, no ensigns of false glory, and scarcely any distinction or precedence, except that which resulted from superior virtue, from the dignity of age or experience, from the sacred office of the priesthood, or from services rendered to the country.

3. The Hebrews, in their primitive state, were separated from the rest of mankind by their religion and laws, and not at all addicted to commerce. They were contented with those arts which belong to a simple and uncultivated state of life. Thus their principal employments were agriculture and the care of cattle.

4. They were, in fact, a nation of husbandmen and shepherds. The lands of Canaan, after the conquest, were parcelled out to the different families. These portions, according to the laws of the country, could not be sold, except for a limited time, and therefore descended to their posterity without diminution.

5. The fruits of the earth, the produce of his hand and labor, constituted the wealth of each individual. Not even the greatest man among the Hebrew nation esteemed it disgraceful to be employed in the lowest offices of rural labor.

6. In the Scripture history, therefore, we read of emi-

CHAPTER XXVIII.—*Questions.*—1. What is said of the domestic life of the Hebrews? 2. Of their equality? 3. Religion and laws? 4. Their lands? 5. The fruits of the earth? 6. Of agriculture, and military service?

nent persons called to the highest and most sacred offices, as generals, kings and prophets, from the plough and from the stalls. All the landed property of the nation was held on the condition of rendering military service to the state: consequently, the nation was one great body of militia, ready at call for the service of the country.

7. Some curious exemptions from service were made, which show the attention of the lawgiver to the agricultural habits and domestic comfort of the people. Thus, a man just married, or one who had newly taken a piece of land into cultivation, was excused from joining the army.

ARABIA.

CHAPTER XXIX.

DESCRIPTION OF ARABIA—THE DESERTS—YEMEN.

1. The great peninsula of Arabia,* which extends from the Gulf of Persia to the Red Sea, and from Syria in the north to the Indian Ocean in the south, forms, as it were, a distinct world, in which man and beast, the

---

* Arabia is noted as the *birthplace of Mahomet*, and the present centre of his worship. It contains several distinct states, those along the coast being addicted to commerce, and bearing a strong resemblance, in manners and customs, to the Turks.

The *Arabs*, the original people of the country, are the descendants of Ishmael, and many of them live a pastoral and wandering life, as did their ancestors, as related in the book of Genesis.

The peninsula of Arabia consists of vast sandy deserts, interspersed with fertile spots. The latter yield many valuable products, as coffee, dates, limes, indigo, &c. The former is the home of the Bedouin Arabs. Here they live, keeping large herds of horses and camels, having tents for dwellings, and roaming

---

7. What were the exemptions from military service?
Chapter XXIX.—*Questions.*—1. Describe Arabia.

DESCRIPTION OF ARABIA. 73

Mahomet.

heavens and the earth, wear a peculiar aspect, and are governed by peculiar laws.

2. Arabia is nearly half as large as the United States of America; but in this great extent of territory, there is no river of any considerable size to water the earth; hardly a mountain to collect the clouds and disperse their contents in rain, or to gather the snows for the refreshment of the burning plains. The face of the earth

from place to place for pasturage or plunder. Their horses are the finest in the world.

Over the sandy plains caravans proceed, laden with rich merchandise, guiding their way by the heavenly bodies. These often fall a prey to the greedy Bedouins, who come and go almost with the swiftness of the eagle.

Mecca, the birthplace of Mahomet, is the capital, and the Holy City of his followers. This is visited by multitudes of pilgrims, every Mahometan being required to go to Mecca once in his life. *Medina* is renowned as containing the tomb of the prophet. *Mocha* is the chief port, on the Red Sea, and is famed for its coffee. *Muscat* has some commerce by sea, and a large trade with the interior by caravans.

2. What of the comparative extent of Arabia, its rivers, mountains, &c. ?

THE DESERTS—YEMEN.

is scorched with almost perpetual drought, and a short-lived vegetation is soon reduced to dust.

3. The winds which sweep across the boundless plains of Arabia, bear along mountains of sand, which constantly threaten to swallow up the works of man, and often bury whole caravans alive. A few springs of water mark, at long intervals, the spots where the life of man and beast may be preserved.

4. Along the coast of the Red Sea, however, there are tracts of land better supplied with water, and here flourishing cities have existed from the earliest antiquity. At the southern extremity of the peninsula, on the shores of the Indian Ocean, is the kingdom of Yemen, in the region called Arabia the Happy.

5. This territory is watered by small streams, and well cultivated. The Coffee-tree is a native of this soil, and here grow spice and incense-bearing shrubs, whose perfumes are said to be wafted out to sea, and to salute the approaching mariner.

6. The race of men who inhabit this region, so unlike every other, are gifted by nature with the vigor and endurance necessary to their condition. The Arab, like his faithful companion, the camel, can endure hunger and thirst to an incredible degree. A few dates, and a little barley, which he moistens with water in his hand, suffice for his nourishment.

7. The northern part of Arabia, bordering on Palestine, had, in ancient times, a numerous population. Here lived the Edomites, the Amalekites, the Cushites; and here is supposed to have been the country of Job. The wanderings of the Israelites led them also through this region. Here is Mount Sinai where the Law was delivered, and here is Mount Nebo where Moses died.

---

3. Its deserts? 4. The coast of the Red Sea? The kingdom of Yemen? 5. What are the productions of Yemen? 6. What is the character of the Arabs? 7. Of Northern Arabia? What nations lived here? What two famous mountains are here?

CHAPTER XXX.

THE TWO RACES OF ARABS—THEIR ORIGIN AND CHARACTER.

1. THE most ancient race of Arabs derive their origin from Heber, who is said to have lived four generations before Abraham. The second race was derived from Ishmael, the son of Abraham and Hagar, of whom it was declared, "His hand shall be against every man, and every man's hand against him."

2. The Arabs boast that their country has never been conquered, while their nation has subdued more than half the Eastern World. Arabia has been, from the earliest ages, ruled by a number of petty princes and lords, independent of each other, and exercising within their own territories a sort of supreme independent power, founded on patriarchal principles.

3. The authority of the father of a family is the first source of government among men, and this influence is still strongly felt among the Arabs. Each little community is considered a family, the head of which is called *sheik* and exercises paternal authority over the rest.

4. The genealogies of the families are carefully reckoned, and the senior branch is always regarded with a high degree of respect and deference. Sometimes a certain form of confederation is made by a great sheik, or *sheik of sheiks*, who holds the supremacy.

5. But each sheik, intrenched in his rocky castle, or roaming with his camels and flocks over the wide expanse of the desert, commonly holds himself independent of every other human power. Individual followers are always ready to resort in considerable numbers to the standard of any successful warrior, who promises daring adventure or rich booty.

6. Hence it is no difficult matter to collect some thousands of freebooters, sufficient to lay under contri-

---

CHAPTER XXX.—*Questions.*—1. From whom are the Arabs derived? 2. What is the boast of the Arabs? 3. What is said of the origin of government? 4. Of the Arab genealogies? 5. Of the Arab sheiks? 6. Of the Arab freebooters?

bution the largest caravans of travellers. On the route between Egypt and Palestine, and the borders of Syria and the Euphrates, large moving encampments of Arabs continually pass to and fro, watching the progress of travellers, ready to avail themselves of any favorable chance for an attack.

7. During the whole of that long era which belongs to ancient history, Arabia preserved its primitive manners and pastoral state, while it had no connexion with foreign nations, except such as rose out of commerce or robbery. This nation also preserved its independence unaffected by those great events which changed the fate of the surrounding nations.

8. It was not till the seventh century of the Christian era, that after a sudden and remarkable revolution, the Arabs issued from their burning deserts with a mighty impulse to change the destinies of a great part of the world.

CHAPTER XXXI.

ANCIENT RELIGION OF THE ARABS—BIRTH OF MAHOMET.

1. The ancient religion of the Arabs was the Sabean form of idolatry, which consisted of the worship of the sun, moon and planets; but long before the birth of Mahomet, they were distracted by a great variety of creeds. Some adhered to the faith of their ancestors; others embraced Judaism, and others Christianity.

2. Mahomet was born at Mecca, A. D. 569. This city is believed by the Arabs to have been founded by Adam. It contained a temple supposed to have been built by Abraham. The early prosperity of Mecca was ascribed to Ishmael, who, according to the Arabian tradi-

---

7. What is said of the primitive state of the Arabs? 8. When did the Arabs issue from their deserts?
Chapter XXXI.—*Questions.*—1. What was the ancient religion of the Arabs? 2. What is said of Mahomet and Mecca?

EARLY LIFE OF MAHOMET.

tions, fixed his residence here. In the temple at Mecca was a black stone, called the *Kaaba*, which was believed to have fallen from heaven, and was therefore the object of superstitious veneration.

3. Mahomet's father was an idolater. His mother was a Jewess, who had been converted to Christianity; and from her instructions he probably derived the religious impressions for which he was distinguished even in boyhood. Both his parents died while he was yet a child, and Mahomet was left to the care of his uncle.

4. In early life, he engaged in trade, and went with the Arab caravan to Syria. Afterwards, he attached himself to the household of a rich widow, named Kadijah. She was so well pleased with his talents for business, as well as his handsome figure, that she gave him her hand in marriage, and made him master of her splendid fortune.

5. Every year he spent a month in retirement in a cave near Mecca, where he devoted himself to meditation and prayer. His travels, as a merchant, had made him acquainted with the principal forms of religion then existing in the East. In Syria, he found Christians of various sects, Jews, Magians and Sabeans.

6. Arabia presented to him many varieties of idolatry, and exiles from Persia informed him of the doctrines of Zoroaster and Mani. A singular dream led him to believe that he was chosen by the Deity to reconcile all these jarring creeds, and to unite mankind in the worship of the one true God. In the solitude of the cave, he dreamed that the angel Gabriel appeared to him and hailed him as a prophet.

---

3. Of Mahomet's family and early life? 4. His travels and marriage? 5. His meditations on religion? 6. His dream?

CHAPTER XXXII.

PREACHING OF MAHOMET—THE HEGIRA.

1. Under the delusion inspired by this dream, Mahomet announced himself as the preacher of a new religion. He first made a convert of his wife, and then of his friends and relations. These converts were called *Mussulmans;* that is, persons resigned to the divine will. Their faith was confirmed by revelations which Mahomet pretended to receive from Gabriel.

2. But at first the progress of the new religion was slow. Mahomet preached in the market-place of Mecca. The officers of the city opposed his doctrine, which threatened to destroy the influence which they derived from the worship of the Kaaba. Several of the Mussulmans were forced, by persecution, to abandon their homes and seek refuge in Abyssinia.

3. But Mahomet was not dismayed; and when he was advised to suspend his preaching for a season, he replied, "Were my enemies to place the sun on my right hand, and the moon on my left, they would not persuade me to change my course."

4. The enemies of Mahomet, unable to silence him, laid a plot for his assassination, and he was compelled to save himself by flight. In the dead of the night, with a single companion, he left his house and stole out of the city.

5. They concealed themselves for three days in a cavern not far from Mecca. Their pursuers came to the cave, but seeing a spider's web over the entrance, and a pigeon's nest near it, they concluded that no human being was in that neighborhood, and turned away.

6. The companion of Mahomet was struck with terror at this danger. "We are but two," said he. "There

---

Chapter XXXII.—*Questions.*—1. How did Mahomet announce himself? What were his followers called? 2. What progress did he make? 3. What declaration? 4. What was done by his enemies? 5. What happened in a cave? 6. Where did Mahomet find refuge?

is a third," replied Mahomet: "it is God himself." From this cavern the fugitives directed their course to Medina, where they were favorably received, as some of the most eminent citizens of that place had been converted during their visits to Mecca.

7. This event is called the *Hegira*, or flight. It occurred in the year 622; and from this epoch the Mahometans compute their chronological reckonings, as we compute from the birth of Christ.

CHAPTER XXXIII.

SUCCESS OF MAHOMET—HIS DEATH.

1. Converts to the doctrine of Mahomet now flocked to Medina, and were formed into warlike bands; these infested all the roads to Mecca, and took vengeance for the insult offered to their master. The plunder was shared equally among the soldiers, and their courage was stimulated by success.

2. Warriors from all parts of Arabia were soon attracted hither by the hope of wealth and glory. In a battle near the well of Beder, the forces of Mahomet were on the point of being defeated, when he stooped down, took up a handful of dust, and flung it toward the enemy, exclaiming, "May their faces be confounded!" This simple action revived the enthusiasm of his followers, and they gained a decisive victory, which he failed not to ascribe to a divine interposition.

3. Mahomet now undertook to propagate his doctrine by the sword, and began by persecuting the Jews because they would not receive him as their Messiah. He soon became the most powerful chief in Arabia, and his disciples received his words as the inspired oracles of God. The instructions which he delivered were written down by them on palm-leaves and shoulder-blades of mutton, for Mahomet himself was unable

---

7. What is the Hegira?
Chapter XXXIII.—*Questions.*—1. What was the success of Mahomet at Medina? 2. What happened at the well of Beder? What was the effect of this? 3. What did Mahomet now undertake? What is said of Mahomet's disciples and instructions? The Koran?

to read or write. The whole collection of his sayings afterwards received the name of the *Koran* or book.

4. Feeling his power now established, he sent ambassadors, summoning the most powerful monarchs of the earth to become his disciples. The people of Mecca were compelled to let him return to that city, and the authority of Mahomet was soon established throughout all Arabia.

5. But in the midst of his success, he was poisoned by a Jewess, who wished to put his supernatural powers to a trial. He escaped immediate death, but contracted a lingering disease, which brought him to an end in the year 632 A. D. At the time of his death, his followers amounted to one hundred thousand warriors, independent of women, slaves, and other attendants.

CHAPTER XXXIV.

PROGRESS OF THE MAHOMETANS — THEIR MODE OF WARFARE.

1. The disciples of Mahomet were overwhelmed with despair at the death of their master. Omar, a fiery zealot, drawing his sword, declared that he would strike off the head of the man who should dare to say that the prophet was no more.

2. But Abu Beker, the faithful friend and earliest disciple of Mahomet, addressing Omar and the multitude, said : " Is it Mahomet or the God of Mahomet, that we worship ? The God of Mahomet lives forever, but his prophet was a mortal like ourselves, and as he had predicted to us, he has undergone the common lot of humanity."

3. By these words the tumult was appeased, and Abu Beker was chosen *Khalif* or successor to the prophet.

---

4. Of the establishment of his authority? 5. How did he come to his end?

CHAPTER XXXIV.—*Questions.*—1. What happened after the death of Mahomet? 2. What was done by Abu Beker? 3. Who was the first khalif?

The wonderful revolution, which, during the life of Mahomet, had been confined to Arabia, made a wide and rapid progress under his successors.

4. Mahomet had founded his military system entirely upon the confident belief with which he had inspired his warriors, that whoever died in battle was sure of eternal happiness. But he made no change in the Arab manner of fighting. The soldiers were half naked, armed, when on foot, only with bows and arrows; when on horseback with a light lance and a sabre.

5. Their horses were unequalled in the world for their powers of endurance, their docility and their spirit. But they did not act in large or regular masses; they knew nothing of those manœuvres and charges practised by modern cavalry, which bear down battalions by their resistless weight. Single warriors advanced in front of the army to signalize themselves by acts of personal prowess, and after a few strokes from their flashing cimeters, escaped from their enemies by the swiftness of their steeds.

6. Battles were long-continued skirmishes, and frequently lasted for several days. It was not till after their adversaries, exhausted by fatigue, were put to the rout, that the Arabs became terrible in pursuit. They do not seem to have made any progress in military science during the early and most brilliant period of the Mussulman conquests. There was no sort of warlike engine in their armies; and they besieged a city in the manner of savages.

7. Mahomet did not connect any political opinions with his religion. He did nothing to destroy the freedom of the desert. He instituted no aristocratical distinction nor hereditary power, either in his own or any other family. When he died, no organization had been given to the Mussulman empire.

8. The enthusiasm he had created, existed among his followers, and each man believed that his sword, his wealth and his power ought to have no other destination

---

4. How was the military system of Mahomet founded? 5. What is said of the Arab horses? 6. What of their battles? 7. What is said of Mahomet's political opinions? 8. What of the enthusiasm of the Arabs?

than that of extending the knowledge of the true Deity. They adopted, therefore, as a war-cry, the words,—"There is no god but God, and Mahomet is his prophet!"

CHAPTER XXXV.

CONQUEST OF PERSIA BY THE SARACENS.

Saracen army on the march.

1. THE khalif soon found it necessary to provide employment for the restless and energetic spirits by which he was surrounded. An army was sent to invade Syria, then under the dominion of the emperor of Constantinople. The invaders captured Bosra and laid siege to Damascus. It was now that they became known to the Christian world under the title of *Saracens*, which means robbers or marauders.

CHAPTER XXXV.—*Questions.*—1. How did the Arabs obtain the name of Saracens?

2. The Greek emperor Heraclius sent an army of 100,000 men to relieve Damascus, but this force was defeated, and the rich and beautiful capital of Syria fell into the hands of the Saracens. Abu Beker died on the day of this capture, and Omar was chosen his successor.

3. The Kingdom of Persia was already singled out for invasion by the Saracens. Kaled, surnamed the *Sword of God*, led an army across the desert to the banks of the Euphrates. The Persians, distracted by internal troubles, made but a feeble resistance. A great battle was fought at Cadesia, A. D. 636, where the Persian army was overthrown.

4. The king, Yezdijird, fled to the mountains of Media, and the conquerors took possession of the royal capital, Ctesiphon. An immense quantity of rich booty fell into their hands; but the ignorant Arabs could not estimate the value of their acquisition. Many of them had never seen gold, and when they found large quantities of it among their plunder, went round offering it for sale, and saying, "I will give any quantity of this yellow metal for a little silver."

5. Persia was completely subdued by the Saracens. The king, Yezdijird, wandered among the mountains and deserts for ten years, and was at length murdered by a miller, with whom he had taken shelter. The royal capital, with its magnificent palace, was permitted to fall to ruins, and travellers are now unable to identify the spot.

6. Within twenty years after the death of Mahomet, his followers had subdued and converted the people of all that wide extent of territory lying between the river Tigris and the Caspian Sea.

---

2. What is said of Damascus? 3. Of the kingdom of Persia? 4. What happened at the capture of Ctesiphon? 5. What became of Yezdijird? 6. What was the extent of the Mahometan conquests within twenty years?

CHAPTER XXXVI.

CONQUEST OF SYRIA AND EGYPT.

The Khalif Omar orders the Alexandrian Library to be burnt.

1. In the mean time, the Saracens were pursuing their successful career in Syria and Palestine. City after city surrendered to their armies, and Abu Obeidah, the lieutenant of the khalif, laid siege to Jerusalem. After four months, the city was compelled to surrender, and Omar went in person to receive the submission of Jerusalem, which the Mahometans as well as the Christians have always regarded as a holy city.

2. The equipage of the khalif was characteristic of the simplicity that still prevailed among the Saracens. He rode upon a red camel, with a sack of corn and a cruise of water slung from his saddle to supply his wants during the journey. A wooden platter was the only utensil he carried with him. His dress

---

CHAPTER XXXVI.—*Questions.*—1. What is said of the conquest of Jerusalem? 2. Of the equipage of the khalif?

was of camel's hair, coarse and torn, and a single servant constituted his retinue.

3. In this guise he reached the Saracen camp, where he recited the public prayers and preached a sermon to the troops. He then signed the capitulation, securing to the Christians of Jerusalem protection in person, property and religious worship, on the payment of a moderate tribute, after which he entered the city in triumph, A. D. 637.

4. On the spot where Solomon's temple had stood Omar ordered a magnificent mosque to be erected, which is standing at this day. Within six years after their first appearance in Syria, the Saracens completed the conquest of the whole of that province including Palestine.

5. They next invaded Egypt and subdued it with little difficulty. Alexandria alone made a vigorous defence; but it was finally taken by storm, and its valuable library was consigned to the flames by the fanatical Omar, who was ignorant of literature and science.

6. It is said that the number of books was so great, that they were employed for six months as fuel in heating the baths of the city. But the whole story of the destruction of this library is doubted by many historians.

CHAPTER XXXVII.

CONQUEST OF SPAIN—DECLINE AND FALL OF THE SARACEN EMPIRE.

1. From Egypt the Saracens pursued their victorious career westward, and by the close of the seventh century, the whole of the north-east of Africa had submitted to their arms and religion.

2. The Mauritanians, in the country now called Mo-

---

3. Of the capitulation of Jerusalem? 4. What was built on the foundation of Solomon's temple? 5. What is said of the conquest of Egypt? 6. Of the destruction of the Alexandrian library?

CHAPTER XXXVII.—*Questions.*—1. What is said of north-eastern Africa? 2. Of the Mauritanians?

86 DECLINE AND FALL OF THE SARACEN EMPIRE.

rocco, offered a fierce resistance to the invaders; but they were finally subdued. These people strongly resembled the Arabs in their manners, habits and complexion, and the name of Arab was here lost in that of *Moor*.

3. From Mauritania, the invaders passed over into Spain, where they overthrew Roderick, the Gothic king of that country, and established their dominion in those parts of the peninsula bordering on the Mediterranean. This continued till 1492 A. D. Not content with their success, the Moors crossed the Pyrenees, and proceeded northward through France to the Loire.

4. They even meditated a plan of conquest which would have subjected all Christendom to their yoke. They proposed to conquer France, Italy and Germany, and then, descending the Danube, to overthrow the empire of Constantinople.

5. But the French, under Charles Martel, checked them in their career, and at the great battle of Tours, which lasted seven days, the Saracens were overthown, with a loss of 300,000 men, A. D. 732. This was the most important victory ever gained in Europe, as it rescued all Christendom from the Mahometan yoke.

6. The Khalif Omar was succeeded by Othman, under whom the Saracens conquered Armenia, Nubia, Cyprus and Rhodes. The celebrated brazen statue in the latter island, known as the Colossus, was broken to pieces and sold to a Jew, who loaded 900 camels with the fragments.

7. The death of Othman, who fell, like Omar, by assassination, caused a revolt among the Saracens. Ali and Moawiyah, the rival khalifs, filled the Mahometan empire with tumult. The latter founded a new dynasty called the *Ommiades*.

8. The empire was dismembered by these intestine divisions, and the Ommiades were encountered by another dynasty called the *Abbassides*, and a third called the *Fatimites*. The first was distinguished by a white flag, the second by a black, and the third by a green one.

---

3. Of the Saracenic invasion of Spain and France? 4. Their scheme of universal conquest? 5. What great defeat did they sustain? 6. What is said of the Colossus of Rhodes? 7. What of the new dynasty of the Saracens? 8. What names and badges did the different dynasties assume?

DECLINE AND FALL OF THE SARACENIC EMPIRE. 87

9. The contentions of these rivals caused a fearful amount of bloodshed and desolation. Their separation from each other was soon followed by other schisms—that of the Edrissites of Mauritania, and the Aglobites of Eastern Africa.

Scheherazade telling the stories of the Arabian Nights.

10. Bagdad, founded by the Khalif Al Mansur, became the capital of the Abbasside dynasty. The khalifs of this line were generous patrons of science, literature and the arts, especially Haroun Al Raschid, the hero of the Arabian Nights, and his son, Al Mamoun. The love of learning spread from Bagdad into the other Saracenic countries. The Ommiade khalifs founded universities in Spain, the Fatimites established schools in Egypt, and the Mahometan nations were distinguished for their attainments in science, while Christian Europe remained sunk in barbarism.

11. The Saracenic empire gradually passed from splendor into weakness, and Turkish mercenary troops were maintained in large numbers by the later khalifs. These became, in course of time, the masters of their

---

9. What is said of their dissensions? 10. Of the khalifs of Bagdad? 11. Of the decline and fall of the Saracenic empire?

sovereigns, and the dignity of khalif, after having long been an empty title, was finally abolished, A. D. 1258.

CHAPTER XXXVIII.

THE WAHABEES.

1. By the time the Saracens had formed a new and powerful empire out of the material of their conquests, the rude rocks and deserts of Arabia had ceased to be regarded as a fit residence for the opulent and ambitious khalifs. The capital of this great dominion being removed to Bagdad, in the rich plain of Mesopotamia, Arabia was left to herself, and resumed her natural and original character.

2. She was thus detached from other countries, and her inhabitants no longer dreamed of foreign conquests, but returned to their pristine state of rude and roving freedom. When the Turks carried their victorious arms into the south, they infested the coast of the Red Sea, and took possession of the western ports of Arabia as far as Mocha.

3. But after maintaining their footing here for two centuries, the decline of their power enabled the Arabian sheiks to regain their independence.

4. During the 18th century, Arabia became the scene of another religious revolution. A prophet of obscure birth, named Abd ul Wahab, made his appearance about the year 1720, and attracted numerous followers. His first object appears to have been a reform of the Mahometan religion, by discarding the traditions which had been engrafted upon it, and denouncing the practice of paying divine honors to any human being, even to Mahomet.

5. His followers were called *Wahabees*. One of them, named Ibn Saoud, was a warlike and powerful

---

CHAPTER XXXVIII.—*Questions.*—1. What happened after the establishment of the Saracenic empire? 2. What effect had this change upon Arabia? 3. What is said of the Arab sheiks? 4. Who was Abd ul Wahab? What was his object? 5. Who was Ibn Saoud? What became of the tomb of Mahomet?

prince, who attempted to propagate this doctrine by the sword. He captured the sacred cities of Mecca and Medina, destroyed the tomb of Mahomet, and became master of a large portion of Arabia.

6. The Turkish government was thrown into great alarm by his successes, and at length prevailed upon Mehemet Ali, the pasha of Egypt, to undertake the subjugation of this dangerous rebel. Mehemet and his son Ibrahim invaded Arabia and recaptured the sacred cities, A. D. 1812.

7. The Wahabee leaders were taken prisoners or put to death, and their forces dispersed. But large numbers of these sectaries still lurk in the desert, watching a favorable moment for raising again the standard of religious reformation in Arabia.

CHAPTER XXXIX.

THE MAHOMETAN RELIGION.

1. The religion of Mahomet does not consist in belief and dogmas alone, but in the practice of morality, in justice and charity. Almsgiving is prescribed as a rigorous duty, and each believer is required to bestow a tenth of his income upon the poor.

2. Five times a day the Mussulman is bound to utter a short and fervent prayer, in words of his own, without any set form. As a means of fixing his attention, he is commanded to turn his face towards Mecca when he prays.

3. Personal cleanliness is also a duty of every true believer in Mahomet. Washing the face and hands is a necessary preparation for every prayer. Yet, as this doctrine was first proclaimed to a people who dwelt in deserts, where water was not always to be found, the Koran permits the faithful, in case of extreme need, to use sand.

---

6. What was done by the Turkish government and Mehemet Ali? 7. What was the fate of the Wahabees?

Chapter XXXIX.—*Questions.*—1. What are the principles of the religion of Mahomet? 2. What is said of the Mahometan prayers? 3. Of cleanliness?

4. The Mahometan fasts are rigid, and admit of no exception. Wine and other intoxicating liquors are forbidden at all times and in all places. During the festival of the Ramadan, which may happen at any season of the year, the Mussulman, from sun-rise to sun-set, must abstain from meat, drink, the bath, and all other sensual gratifications. Swine's flesh is prohibited as rigidly in the Mahometan as in the Jewish code, and every believer is required to make a pilgrimage, once in his life, to Mecca.

5. But in spite of the simplicity of the Mahometan creed, it has been found impossible to preserve anything like unanimity of sentiment among the various nations that profess it. The Mussulman sects have been as numerous and violent as those of any other religion.

6. The two most important sects, at present, are the *Sunnees* and the *Sheahs*. The former call themselves the orthodox party, and stigmatize their opponents as heretics. The Persians have been of the Sunnee sect for the last three hundred years.

7. The spirit of hostility which exists among the Mahometan sectaries is rancorous and irreconcilable. Names which are never mentioned but with blessings by one party, are hourly cursed by another.

8. The religion founded by Mahomet has had a vast influence upon mankind. Many persons have doubted whether this remarkable man was a mere fanatic, sincerely and blindly believing the doctrines which he preached, or whether he was an ingenious and successful hypocrite. Probably he was a mixture of both.

9. The Koran appears to have been composed with some knowledge of the Bible; but it is a work utterly without order, and full of extravagant absurdities and contradictions. The Mahometans believe in the Old Testament, but have not an equal regard for the New.

10. They believe that Mahomet was the last of the prophets; that his name is written on all the gates of

---

4. Of fasts? Of the Ramadan? 5. What is said of the Mussulman sects? 6. Of the Sunnees and Sheahs? 7. Of Mahometan hostilities? 8. What has been the influence of Mahometanism upon mankind? 9. What is said of the Koran? 10. What opinion is entertained of Mahomet?

paradise; that the devil was cast out at his birth; that he visited the seven heavens; that he performed three thousand miracles; that he cleft the moon in two; that fountains of water gushed from his fingers; that celestial spirits obeyed him, and that the angel of death could not take his soul till he had first asked his permission.

11. "The sword," says Mahomet, in the Koran, "is the key of heaven and hell. A drop of blood spent in the cause of God, or a night spent in arms, is of more avail than two months passed in fasting and prayer. Whoever falls in battle, his sins are forgiven: at the day of judgment his words shall be resplendent as vermilion and odoriferous as musk: the loss of limbs shall be supplied with the wings of angels and of cherubims."

12. Mahomet promised the joys of heaven to all who fell in his cause, and he made those joys exceedingly captivating to an Arabian imagination. To each man is assigned seventy beautiful wives—a tent of incomparable costliness—a prodigious number of servants—the choicest wines in golden goblets—the most delicious food—the most sumptuous dresses, and renovated youth, enduring forever. But unbelievers he threatened with torments as lasting and terrible as the joys of heaven are desirable.

---

11. What saying is recorded of him? 12. What promises did he make to his followers?

PHŒNICIA.

CHAPTER XL.

THE ANCIENT PHŒNICIANS—SIDON AND TYRE.

Phœnician Ships passing the Pillars of Hercules.

1. Ancient Phœnicia* lay on the eastern shore of the Mediterranean, having Syria on the north and east, and Palestine on the south. This territory was of very small extent, but well situated for commerce by sea.

2. The Phœnicians appear to have been the descendants of the ancient Canaanites. They were settled on

---

* The territory of ancient Phœnicia is now absorbed in Syria, its ancient title being no longer applied to it. Its cities of Tyre and Sidon, once so famous, are now insignificant places.

Chapter XL.—*Questions.*—1. Describe Phœnicia. 2 From whom were the Phœnicians descended?

this coast before the arrival of the Israelites. The maritime position of their country and its abundance of timber, led them to the practice of ship-building at an early period, and then to navigation and trade beyond sea.

3. They also excelled in useful and beautiful manufactures, so that fabrics of a superior quality were called Sidonian, from Sidon, one of the chief Phœnician cities. The Phœnicians are said to have been the first people who used rudders and sails, and steered their ships at night by the stars.

4. They were also believed to have been the inventors of arithmetic. The Greeks obtained the letters of their alphabet from this country. The Phœnicians also discovered the mode of making glass. They were famous for dyeing cloth of a purple color, the material for which was obtained from a species of shell-fish found on their coast.

5. The commerce of the Phœnicians was extended far and wide by the establishment of colonies in various quarters of Europe and Africa. They obtained gold and silver from Spain, tin from Britain, amber from the Baltic, and copper and iron from the shores of the Black Sea.

6. The earliest historical information respecting this country shows it to have been divided into a number of separate governments. Most of the Phœnician cities and towns were independent states, some of which were governed by kings.

7. Sidon or Zidon was the oldest of these cities, and one of the earliest places in the world that carried on an extensive commerce. Tyre was built by the Sidonians, and became the rival of Sidon and the chief city of Phœnicia.

8. Tyre is the only Phœnician city whose history can be satisfactorily traced. The first king of Tyre was Abibal, who reigned about the year 1050 B. C., and was contemporary with king David. His son and successor,

---

3. What is said of their manufactures, ships, &c. ? 4. Of arithmetic, letters, &c. ? 5. Their commerce ? 6. What was the ancient condition of the country ? 7. What is said of Sidon ? 8. Tyre ? Its kings ? Its commerce ?

Hiram, was the ally of David and his son Solomon. During the reign of Hiram, Tyre acquired a supremacy in Phœnicia, and became the most flourishing emporium of commerce in the ancient world.

CHAPTER XLI.

WAR OF NEBUCHADNEZZAR—CONQUEST OF TYRE BY ALEXANDER.

1. The most remarkable successors of Hiram were Ethbaal I., the father of Jezebel, the wife of Ahab, and Pygmalion, who murdered Sichæus, the husband of Dido, and compelled that princess to escape to Africa, where she founded the city of Carthage.

2. The Tyrians exercised their supremacy over the surrounding cities with so much cruelty, that the Phœnicians applied for protection to the Assyrians, and afterwards to the Babylonians. When attacked by the Assyrians, the people of Tyre defended themselves so courageously, that the assailants were compelled to retire, leaving the city uninjured.

3. Nebuchadnezzar next made war upon Tyre, and laid close siege to the city. He so exhausted it by a constant blockade, that nearly all the inhabitants abandoned the place, and erected another city on a neighboring island, to which they gave the name of New Tyre.

4. A short time after this event, the government was changed; the royal authority was abolished, and annual magistrates, called *Shophetim* or judges, were elected. Their office was somewhat similar to that of the consuls of Rome. The new city, however, never rose to the importance of Old Tyre.

5. After the conquest of Babylon by Cyrus, the Phœnician cities submitted, without resistance, to the Persian

---

Chapter XLI.—*Questions.*—1. What is said of Ethbaal I.? 2. What was the conduct of the Tyrians? 3. Of Nebuchadnezzar? 4. What was the government of Tyre? 5. What is said of the Persians in Phœnicia?

arms, but were permitted to govern themselves according to their own forms. The authority of the king was restored at Tyre, and that city supplied the greater part of the naval force employed by the Persians in their wars with the Greeks.

6. Alexander the Great captured Tyre, after a siege of seven months, B. C. 331. Phœnicia, after this period, became attached to the Macedonian and Syrian monarchies, and never rose to the dignity of an independent government.

7. The Phœnicians preceded the Greeks in forming commercial establishments on the coast of Asia Minor and the shores of the Black Sea. Their colonies proceeded from east to west, along the Mediterranean, occupying the principal islands. Cyprus, Sicily and Sardinia received their settlements, after which they ventured outside the straits, and founded the city of Gades, now Cadiz, in Spain.

8. Their colonies in Northern Africa, such as Leptis, Carthage, Utica, &c., attained to greater splendor than any of the other Phœnician cities, and rivalled Tyre itself in wealth and magnificence. In the Eastern seas, they formed establishments on the Red Sea and the Persian Gulf. By land, they carried on trade with Arabia, Egypt, India, Babylon, Armenia and Scythia.

---

6. Of the conquest by Alexander? 7. Of the Phœnician commercial establishments? 8. Colonies?

SYRIA.

CHAPTER XLII.

HISTORICAL SKETCH.

SYRIANS.

1. This country* extends from the eastern shore of the Mediterranean to the river Euphrates and the Syrian desert. By the Greeks it was regarded as including Palestine and Phœnicia; and so it is considered by its present masters, the Turks. The chief divisions, in ancient times, were Syria Proper and Cælo-Syria, or Hol-

---

* Syria, under the Turkish dominion, embraces Palestine and Phœnicia. *Damascus*, is still a fine city, and is one of the few places that has flourished in ancient and modern times. Aleppo is a large city; Antioch has greatly declined. The ruins of Palmyra and Balbec, in this territory, excite the wonder of every beholder. The former is interesting from the history of its celebrated queen Zenobia, and the latter from its splendid temple of the sun.

Chapter XLII.—*Questions.*—1. Describe Syria.

low Syria, the latter country being situated in a valley between the ranges of Mount Lebanon. The lofty summits of these mountains are capped with perpetual snow, and they were long noted for the magnificent forests of cedars, of which only a few groves now remain.

2. The most ancient inhabitants of Syria are supposed to have been the Aramites, or the descendants of Aram, the youngest son of Shem. In the early scripture times, this country was divided into several small states or kingdoms, the most ancient of which appears to have been Zobah.

3. Saul, king of Israel, overthrew this kingdom, and that of Damascus arose on its ruins. Benhadad II., one of the kings of Damascus, adorned the city with fine buildings, and did much for the glory of the kingdom. After his death, he was worshipped by the Syrians as a god. The kingdom of Damascus was overthrown by Tiglath Pileser, king of Assyria, B. C. 740.

4. Syria was absorbed into the Assyrian monarchy by this conquest. Afterwards, the Persians exercised dominion over it. Alexander the Great subdued it with the rest of the Persian empire, and at his death, it fell into the possession of Seleucus, one of his generals. He erected it into a kingdom, built the city of Antioch for a capital, and founded the dynasty of the *Seleucidæ*, which retained possession of the throne of Syria for nearly two centuries and a half.

5. In the year 64 B. C., Pompey the Great conquered Syria, and reduced the country to a Roman province. Under the Roman emperors, Syria was one of the most flourishing and luxurious provinces of the East. It was the seat of a great commerce, and formed the emporium which connected the eastern countries with Europe.

6. Syria was the first foreign country invaded by the Mahometans, who conquered it with great ease, and thus it became annexed to the Saracen empire. Shortly after this conquest, the Saracen khalif removed his court from Medina to Damascus, and this city became the capital of the empire till it was transferred to Bagdad in the year 749.

---

2. Its ancient inhabitants. 3. What is said of Damascus? 4. Of Alexander, Seleucus, &c.? 5. Of Pompey? 6. Of the Mahometan conquest?

7. At the commencement of the crusades, the European armies invaded and overran this country, but were ultimately expelled by the Saracens. The Mamelukes of Egypt next established their dominion here, and finally, in the year 1516, the Turkish sultan, Selim I., conquered Syria, and annexed it to the Ottoman empire, in which condition it remains at present.

ASIA MINOR.

CHAPTER XLIII.

GENERAL VIEW OF ASIA MINOR—EARLY HISTORY.

1. ASIA MINOR, now under the government of Turkey, is a large peninsula, forming the most western division of Asia. Its shores are washed by the waters of the Mediterranean and Euxine seas. It is almost completely separated from the main continent of Asia by chains of lofty and almost impassable mountains and barren wastes, which closely bar the broad isthmus by which these portions of territory are joined.

2. This country presents a remarkable diversity of soil and climate. The interior is completely encompassed with a girdle of lofty mountains, which enclose a vast hollow into which the waters of many large rivers are poured. This region exhibits an immense range of pasture, on which feed numerous flocks of sheep, droves of horses and herds of goats, while the inhabitants lead nearly the same irregular pastoral life which prevails among the Tartar hordes.

3. The country between the mountains and the sea presents a different and more smiling aspect. The western parts are remarkable for their fertility and their genial climate. In the early ages of history, Asia Minor comprised many distinct kingdoms, the boundaries

---

7. Of the crusades? Of the Mamelukes, &c.?
CHAPTER XLIII.—*Questions.*—1. Describe Asia Minor. 2. Its soil and climate. 3. The western parts.

and divisions of which varied with their political revolutions.

4. Civilization commenced at an early period in this country; its commerce was extensive and flourishing; it contained many large and opulent cities adorned by temples, palaces and other public buildings, which were among the finest pieces of architecture ever erected. The Phœnicians founded colonies on the southern shores of Asia Minor at a very early period.

5. Subsequently, the Greeks settled on the shores of the Ægean Sea. The Greek language and literature were extensively cultivated here, and the fame of the philosophers, historians, poets and artists of this country has descended to our own times.

CHAPTER XLIV.

THE KINGDOMS OF TROY AND PHRYGIA.

1. The three kingdoms of Asia Minor which attract the most notice in ancient history, are Troy, Phrygia and Lydia. The history of Troy consists of traditions preserved by the Greek poets. The city of Troy or Ilium, is said to have been founded by Dardanus, a Samothracian, about 1400 years before Christ.

2. The Trojan war is the most famous event in all Grecian history. It is said to have been caused by Paris, the son of king Priam, of Troy, who stole the wife of king Menelaus, of Sparta. To avenge this wrong, all the Greek states combined in a league and made war upon Troy.

3. After a siege of ten years, the city was taken and destroyed. This event forms the subject of Homer's Iliad—the oldest composition now existing in the Greek language.

---

4. What is said of civilization and commerce here? 5. Of the Greeks of Asia Minor?

Chapter XLIV.—*Questions.*—1. What is said of the early history of Troy? 2. Of the Trojan war? 3. Of the capture of Troy and the Iliad?

4. The history of Phrygia is also composed of obscure traditions. The inhabitants of this country were among the first settlers of Asia Minor. They were civilized at an early period, and were skilful in agriculture and the working of mines. They were also famous for their love of dancing and music.

5. The Phrygians worshipped a deity named *Cybele*, who seems to have been a personification of the prolific powers of the earth. Her priests were named *Corybantes*, and were celebrated for their frantic dances, in which they beat and cut themselves.

6. Most of the Phrygian kings were named either Midas or Gordius. The most celebrated Midas is said to have received from Bacchus the power of turning everything he touched into gold; but finding himself in danger of starving, because his food became gold as soon as he touched it, he prayed to the god to take back his gift.

7. The first Gordius was originally a peasant, and when raised to the throne he consecrated a cart to the gods. The beam was fastened to the yoke by an artfully complicated knot; and a traditional oracle declared that whoever untied the knot should be sovereign of all Asia. Alexander the Great, finding it impossible to untie it, cut the knot with his sword. Hence we have the phrase—"*to cut the Gordian knot.*" After many revolutions, Phrygia became united to the Lydian empire.

CHAPTER XLV.

THE KINGDOM OF LYDIA—IONIA.

1. LYDIA was an interior region: its most ancient name was *Mæonia*. The Lydians were the first people in the world who are known to have coined money. They were, at one time, the most wealthy as well as the most luxurious and effeminate people of Asia.

---

4. What is said of the early history of Phrygia? 5. Of the Phrygian worship? 6. What story is told of Midas? 7. Of Gordius? What was the Gordian knot?

CHAPTER XLV.—*Questions.*—1. What is said of the ancient Lydians?

THE KINGDOM OF LYDIA.

2. In the reign of Gyges, this kingdom rose to great power; but in the time of his successor, Ardys, Asia Minor was devastated by hordes of barbarians from the north, called *Cimmerians*.

3. These people had been expelled from their own country by the Scythians, and for half a century continued their ravages in the kingdom of Lydia, till at length they were driven out of the country by Alyattes, the grandson of Ardys.

4. This monarch became next involved in war with Cyaxares, king of Media; after a contest of six years, the armies of the two nations met at Thymbra, intending to decide the struggle in a general engagement. But a total eclipse of the sun so terrified both armies, in the midst of the fight, that they separated in consternation, without a victory on either side.

5. This remarkable event took place 601 years before Christ. The eclipse was foretold by Thales, the Greek philosopher of Miletus, and is the first that is recorded as having been calculated by an astronomer.

6. Crœsus, the son and successor of Alyattes, conquered all the Greek states in Asia Minor, and extended his empire on the eastern side as far as the river Halys. The magnificence of his court, at Sardis, attracted visiters from various countries.

7. Crœsus was anxious to entertain philosophers and men of learning from Greece. The illustrious Solon was once his guest. Crœsus demanded of him who he thought the happiest man in the world, expecting to be named himself. But he was much surprised and mortified to find the philosopher regardless of his immense wealth and power.

8. Solon declared to him that no man could be pronounced happy till the end of his career was known. The Lydian monarch was deeply offended with the independent opinions and frank language of the Athenian sage; but before long he had ample reason to admire the wisdom of this great man.

---

2. Of Gyges and Ardys? 3. Of the Cimmerians? 4. What happened at the battle of Thymbra? 5. What was done by Thales? 6. By Crœsus? 7. What happened between him and Solon? 8. What reply was made by Solon?

9. Seduced by the oracle of Delphi, which assured him that by marching across the Halys he would overthrow a great empire, Crœsus made war upon Cyrus, king of Persia, but was defeated and taken prisoner. He then discovered the ambiguous meaning of the oracle, which might signify his own empire as well as that of his rival.

Temple of Diana at Ephesus.

10. Crœsus was sentenced by the Persians to die at the stake, according to the barbarous manners of that age. When placed on the funeral pile, he called to remembrance the words of the wise man of Athens, and exclaimed, "O Solon! Solon!" Cyrus asked the meaning of this invocation, and was so struck by the impressive example of the philosopher's wisdom, that he not only spared the life of Crœsus, but made him his friend and counsellor.

11. The kingdom of Lydia became absorbed into the Persian empire by the victory of Cyrus, and never after-

---

9. What was the result of his war with Persia? 10. What happened to Crœsus at the stake? 11. What became of the kingdom of Lydia?

IONIA—FAMOUS MEN OF ASIA MINOR.

wards had an independent existence. The country, like the rest of Asia Minor, is now subject to the Turks.

12. Ionia was situated on the sea-coast, and was contiguous to Lydia. The people are Greeks, and their history is very interesting. Here was the renowned city of Ephesus, and the temple of Diana, one of the seven wonders of the world. It was 420 feet long, was surrounded by 120 pillars, each 70 feet high, and was 200 years in being built.

13. There were many other states in Asia Minor, whose history would be interesting, but we have not space to detail it here. We may however mention some of the famous people who lived here in former times.

14. Galen, one of the most eminent physicians that ever appeared, was born at Pergamus, 131 A. D. Thales, a noted astronomer, already mentioned, was born at Miletus, 646 B. C. In his time there were seven persons living, called the Seven Wise Men. Of these, Thales was one.

15. Some of the wise sayings of Thales are preserved, as follows: "It is better to adorn the mind than the face: the most difficult thing is to know one's self: the easiest thing is to give advice: if we wish to be good, let us avoid what we blame in others."

16. Apelles, a celebrated painter, lived at Ephesus in the time of Alexander, and painted several portraits of him. One day a shoemaker, on seeing a picture by Apelles, told the artist that a shoe represented in it was not well painted. Apelles saw the fault and corrected it. The shoemaker became conceited and made other criticisms, upon which Apelles said—"A cobbler should not go beyond his last." This became a proverb and is still in use.

17. Diogenes, called the Cynic, on account of his bitter speeches, was a native of Paphlagonia. He lived in the time of Alexander, who paid him a visit. He found the philosopher living in a tub!

---

12. What of Ionia? The Temple of Diana? 14. What of Galen? Thales? 15. Tell some of the wise sayings of Thales. 16. What of Apelles? 17. Diogenes?

TURKEY IN ASIA.*

CHAPTER XLVI.

HISTORY OF THE TURKS.

1. The Turks originated in Tartary, many centuries since. They appear in history as early as the year 500

---

* The Turkish or Ottoman empire, embraces territory in Europe, anciently belonging to the Greek empire, and territories in Asia, formerly belonging to various governments. The centre and capital of this empire is Constantinople, situated on a sea which separates Europe from Asia. Here the sultan or emperor resides.

Turkey in Asia is renowned alike for its fine climate, its rich productions, and its remarkable history. No part of the world is more favored by nature than this. Yet, being subject to the

---

Chapter XLVI.—*Questions.*—1. Where did the Turks originate?

B. C. They seem to have branched into several nations or tribes. In the eleventh century, the Seljukian branch obtained a footing in a part of Persia, where they had a flourishing kingdom for nearly two centuries.

2. A portion of the Seljuks established themselves in Asia Minor, Solyman being their first sovereign. The kingdom was, however, at last reduced to a small inland district. Another branch of Turks, led by Ortogrul, was driven into this quarter, and were received by Aladdin, the chief of the Seljuks, with great favor, A. D. 1280.

3. *Othman* or *Osman*, one of the sons of Ortogrul, succeeded his father, and greatly extended his empire. His history, as given by Turkish writers, is very inter-

---

Turkish government, it is in a degraded and depressed state. The western part of this region, contiguous to Russia in Europe, is called Asia Minor. To the north-east is Armenia. Along the eastern border is Koordistan, the site of ancient Assyria. At the eastern extremity of the Mediterranean are Palestine and Syria; and between these and Koordistan is Mesopotamia where Babylon was situated. The Turks of this region resemble those of Constantinople. Smyrna is the most considerable town of Asia Minor, and has an extensive commerce.

The Armenians are Christians, and are the leading merchants in the cities of Persia, Turkey, and Arabia. The Koords are a fierce and warlike people, who descend from their mountains and plunder the inhabitants of the adjacent regions. In Mesopotamia may still be seen the gloomy and desolate ruins of Babylon, witnesses of the fearful fulfilments of prophecy. Here also are Bagdad on the Tigris, the ancient seat of the khalifs; Mosul near the ruins of ancient Nineveh; and other celebrated places.

In Palestine are still to be traced the scenes of many of the most interesting events in the Bible. Jerusalem is here, but it is greatly changed. The Temple of Solomon is gone, and Turkish mosques lift their minarets over the city. The most superb of these is that of Omar. Many pilgrims resort to Jerusalem, it being regarded as a holy place by Turks and Christians; yet it is degraded from its former splendor, and is now the seat of superstition and priestly imposture. Near to Jerusalem are Bethlehem, Nazareth, &c. In Syria is Damascus, famous in history; and here also are the majestic ruins of Balbec and Palmyra, or Tadmor in the Desert.

What of the Seljukians? 2. What of a portion of the Seljuks? 3. What of Othman?

esting. From him the present Turks, called *Ottomans,* derive their name.

4. The dominion of Othman was extended by his successors, who appear to have been very able and warlike sovereigns. All Asia Minor, Syria, Koordistan and Mesopotamia, one after another, were speedily wrested by the Turks from the Saracens and the Byzantine empire.

5. At last, their armies crossed into Europe, and for a long period, the Turkish armies excited the alarm and terror of Christendom. They took Constantinople in 1453, since which time it has been their capital. They also extended their territories to the north, taking in some of the finest territories which had formerly belonged to the Greek branch of the Roman empire.

6. The Turks adopted the Mahometan religion, and must now be considered as the chief supporters of that faith. They are grave and solemn in their aspect, and have formerly disdained to mingle with Christians or Europeans. But within a few years, they have somewhat relaxed: they are less bigoted in matters of religion, and are adopting some European customs.

7. Fifty years ago it was difficult and dangerous to travel in the remote parts of Turkey, but it is different now. Many people, at the present day, visit even such places as Palestine, Koordistan, &c., for amusement.

8. In 1848, an expedition was sent out by our government to examine the Dead Sea and the vicinity, in Palestine. The waters of this wonderful sea or lake, were found to be very bitter and salt, and so heavy that a copper boat, in passing over it, was severely battered by the waves.

9. No fish were found in the lake, though ducks were seen swimming upon its surface. To the south, is a rocky ridge of salt, five miles long and 150 feet high. Here is a lofty pillar of salt, which the people around call Lot's Wife, and believe it to be "the pillar of salt" into which the wife of the patriarch was changed, as mentioned in the Bible.

---

4. How was the Turkish dominion extended? 5. What happened in 1453? 6. What of the religion and manners of the Turks? 7. What of Turkey at the present day? 8. What of the Dead Sea? 9. The pillar of salt?

ARMENIA.

CHAPTER XLVII.

HISTORICAL SKETCH.

ARMENIANS.

1. ARMENIA is an interior country of Western Asia, lying to the south-east of the Euxine or Black sea. It is a very elevated region, and is traversed by lofty mountains, the summits of which are covered with snow. Hence the climate is very cold. The winters are long and severe. Snow begins to fall in August, and covers the ground from October till March.

2. On the summit of Mount Ararat, in this country, the ark is supposed to have rested after the flood. The Armenians are one of the oldest nations in the world, and have kept themselves distinct from the rest of mankind from the earliest times of which we have any exact

CHAPTER XLVII.—*Questions.*—1. Describe Armenia. 2. What is said of Ararat? What of the antiquity of the Armenians?

knowledge. They are supposed to have been originally of the same race as the primitive Syrians.

3. This country is said to have constituted an independent kingdom in early times, but it afterwards became subject to the Assyrians, the Medes, the Persians, the Greeks and the Syrians. At intervals, during these revolutions, it was governed by its native princes.

4. In the reign of Tigranes, king of Armenia, about a century before Christ, this kingdom attained to its greatest height of power and splendor. Tigranes conquered Syria, Parthia, Phœnicia, and other countries, which he annexed to his empire. This success induced him to assume the proud title of "King of Kings."

5. This powerful monarch, however, became involved in hostilities with the Romans, and the armies of the latter, commanded by Pompey and Lucullus, overthrew the forces of the king of kings. Armenia, however, was allowed to retain its independence.

6. About two hundred years after Christ, the Persians conquered Armenia, but the possession of this kingdom was long disputed between the eastern conquerors and the Greek emperors of Constantinople. At length, the latter established their dominion over it.

7. Afterwards, the Saracens invaded the country. They were followed by the Tartars, the Turks, the Persians and the Russians. These invaders devastated Armenia for many centuries, and finally Armenia was divided between the Russian, Turkish and Persian monarchies.

8. Erzeroom, belonging to the Turkish portion of the country, is the first city in Armenia. Erivan is the capital of Russian Armenia.

9. Armenia was crossed by the celebrated Xenophon and his ten thousand Greeks, who fled after the battle of Cunaxa, in Persia, 400 B. C. Their adventures amid the snows of Armenia, as told by Xenophon, were very remarkable. After the greatest sufferings, they reached Greece in safety. This retreat is very famous in history.

---

3. What was the ancient government of Armenia? 4. What took place in the reign of Tigranes? What title was assumed by this monarch? 5. What was his fate? 6. What was done by the Persians and Greeks in Armenia? 7. By the Saracens? 8. What of Erzeroom? Erivan? 9. Xenophon?

TARTARY.*

CHAPTER XLVIII.

DESCRIPTION OF TARTARY—THE PASTORAL TRIBES.

Tartar encampment.

1. TARTARY is the name which Europeans and Americans give to that immense region extending almost

---

*Tartary is now divided into Independent and Chinese Tartary. It has formerly been the seat of mighty empires, but it is now divided between several tribes, the chief of whom are the *Usbeks* in the south, and *Kirguis* in the north. The climate of this region is mild, and the soil fertile. A portion of the people engage in trade and agriculture, but the greater part of them live by roaming from place to place with their flocks and herds. The men are the finest horsemen in the world. Horse-flesh is a favor-

---

CHAPTER XLVIII.—*Questions.*—1. Describe Tartary.

entirely across Central Asia, from the Caspian Sea to the North Pacific Ocean. This country is marked by the boldest and most strikingly contrasted features. In the east are plains of amazing extent; in the west are long and lofty chains of mountains, supporting very elevated table-lands.

2. In the central part of Tartary is the great Desert of Cobi or Shamo, which is about 2000 miles in circuit. Of this dreary waste very little is known; but according to the account of Marco Polo, the celebrated Venetian traveller, who passed over it on his way to China, more than 500 years ago, it is traversed, like the African desert, by caravans of camels.

3. Many stories were told by this traveller of the terrors and dangers of this journey. In the awful solitude of the desert, the wanderer who chanced to stray from the main body of his companions, imagined that he heard a sound, sometimes like the march of a caravan, sometimes like that of music and warlike instruments, echoing through the air. Following these delusions, he was led out of his course till he was irrecoverably lost.

4. These superstitious terrors were natural to persons who found themselves bewildered in the depths of these gloomy wilds. All the habitable parts of this desert are covered with rank and luxuriant pasture; the rest is composed of shifting sand or dry gravel and pebbles.

---

ite food with the people, and a drink made from mare's milk is greatly esteemed. Courtship is performed on horseback. Both parties being mounted, the lover pursues the object of his affection. She flies for a time, but allows herself to be caught at a proper period. *Khiva* is the great slave market of Tartary. *Samarcand*, the gorgeous capital of the former emperors, is now nearly in ruins. *Bucharia* is a mart for the rich trading caravans, between China and the countries to the west, and, besides, has numerous mosques and colleges devoted to Mahometan learning.

Independent Tartary was the country of Zingis Khan, Tamerlane, &c. These great conquerors, as well as some others of this race, had their capitals here. The Tartars are a vigorous people, and have frequently made conquests in other countries. The Turks, who have established their empire in Europe and Western Asia, are of this stock; and India, China, and Persia, have frequently fallen under Tartar dominion.

---

2. The Desert of Cobi. 3. What story is told of it by Marco Polo? 4. How are these phenomena explained?

THE PASTORAL TRIBES.

5. The climate of this region is in general cold, though some portions enjoy a comparatively mild temperature. Many *oases* or fertile spots are scattered here and there amid the arid waste; and sometimes a considerable extent of country is found susceptible of cultivation.

6. The ancients gave to this vast region the general name of *Scythia*, though they had no means of knowing its actual extent. When first known to Europeans, the inhabitants had already emerged from the hunting state, and supported themselves by pasturage; but the defects in the soil and climate of the country seem to have prevented them from entering on agricultural pursuits.

7. To the inhabitants of a civilized country, the pastoral state suggests pleasing and romantic ideas. The hut of the shepherd seems the abode of innocence, gentleness and rural simplicity. This picture is sometimes not far removed from the truth. But when shepherds are formed into vast assemblages, and led by ambitious chiefs, a very different scene is exhibited to our view, and all the simplicity and romance of a pastoral life disappears.

8. Hence it is that Tartary, which seems to have been, in all ages, remarkable for the rapid increase of the human race, has been the great store-house, out of which Providence has permitted hordes of barbarians to issue forth from time to time, to destroy the old, indolent and worn out nations, occupying the warmer and more genial parts of the earth.

9. It is also a remarkable fact that to Tartary we can trace the origin of most of the prominent nations of the present day. The Chinese, Japanese, Coreans, and a great part of the people of Farther India, are of Mongolian origin; five millions of Siberians are of the same stock; the Turks originally came from Tartary, as well as the progenitors of nearly every nation of Europe. There can be little doubt that the Malays and American Indians were also of Tartar origin.

---

5. What is said of the climate and oases of the desert? 6. What is said of Scythia and its ancient inhabitants? 7. Of the pastoral state? 8. For what has Tartary been remarkable in all ages? What has Providence permitted? 9. What nations trace their origin to Tartary?

CHAPTER XLIX.
THE ANCIENT SCYTHIANS.

1. These rude people, trained to war and the use of arms from infancy, were easily led on to the spoil of happier regions, on which nature had lavished her gifts, and of which the sword seemed to render them the rightful possessors.

2. These ancient contests were marked with barbarity. In rude tribes, the laws of war are always cruel; but the pastoral nations, destitute of all the refinements of civilization, are strangers to humanity and mercy. Even nations whose military code is considered by us as barbarous, speak with horror of Scythian devastation.

3. The series of invasions, therefore, which have poured down from the immense regions of Tartary upon the surrounding countries, have always been numbered among the most dreadful calamities which have afflicted the human race. They have been compared to a scourge

---

Chapter XLIX.—*Questions.*—1. What is said of the ancient Scythians? 2. Their wars? 3. Their invasions?

which the Deity continually holds in his hand to chastise the crimes of mankind.

4. In a rude state of the military art, bodily strength and powers form the leading qualifications. Hence, the Scythians, who lived, as it were, on horseback, and were inured to every vicissitude of the seasons, proved always an overmatch for the effeminate nations of Southern Asia.

5. The great empires of the South were, therefore, often subjected to Scythian or Tartar dynasties; and as these were successively enervated by wealth and luxury, new swarms poured in from the north to occupy their place. But the Roman empire having carried the military art to a perfection before unknown, long resisted and repelled these formidable assailants.

6. The mighty tide of invasion, however, continued to roll on, wars after wars, from the farthest depths of interior Asia, till Rome, with all her greatness and all her glory, was buried beneath it.

7. The barbarians who accomplished these great revolutions had no fixed abode in their own country. They roved continually rom place to place, inhabiting large movable tents conveyed on wagons, driving before them their herds, which were their sole subsistence. Their chief food was horse-flesh, and their only luxury an intoxicating liquor called *koumiss*, which they brewed from mare's milk.

8. The descriptions handed down to us by ancient authors, portray some of these tribes in terrible colors. Of the Huns, it is said, the mothers flattened the noses of their children and gashed their cheeks, to give them a hideous appearance. The people lived on roots or flesh, crushed between the saddle and the back of the horse. They dressed in skins which were permitted to decay upon their limbs. The men ate and drank and held councils on horseback. The women, even, neither feared wounds nor death. They could be seen prowling over the battle-field, in company with the wolf and the raven.

---

4. How did the Scythians live? 5. What is said of the Tartar dynasties? The Roman empire? 6. The Tartar invasions? 7. What was the character of the barbarian conquerors? 8. What is said of the ancient Huns?

CHAPTER L.

CONQUESTS OF ZINGIS KHAN.

1. The Goths, the Alans and the Huns, who ravaged the Roman empire, all proceeded from the vast wilds of Tartary. The Turks, at a later period, issued from the same region, and made irruptions into the dominions of the Byzantine or Greek emperors.

2. After these successive invasions, it might have been expected that an interval of exhaustion would follow, and that the world would enjoy a season of tranquillity. This hope was soon dispelled by the appearance of *Zingis Khan*, the most terrible and mighty destroyer of mankind recorded in history. This daring chief was originally named *Temugin*.

3. He is said to have been first a blacksmith and then a petty leader among the Mongols—a tribe which roamed over the country to the north of China. His countrymen being engaged in a war with their neighbors, elected him for their commander-in-chief. He led them on to victory, and enlisted under his standard the tribes which he subdued.

4. His continued successes in war enabled him to obtain a decided supremacy over all the hordes that occupied the vast deserts of Eastern Tartary. He now assumed the title of Khan or emperor, and exchanged the name of Temugin for that of Zingis, which he rendered the most formidable ever known in the East.

5. At his capital of Karakorum he summoned a general congress of the Tartar hordes, in the year 1205. By their consent, he was formally placed on the throne of the Mongol empire. He made a code of laws for the government of his empire, by which the Tartars were interdicted from all servile labors, and devoted solely to the profession of arms. The occupations of peace were assigned to slaves and strangers.

Chapter L.—*Questions.*—1. What is said of the Goths, Alans, Huns, and Turks? 2. Of Zingis Khan? 3. What was his early life? 4. What is said of his successes? 5. What was done by him at Karakorum? What laws did he make?

6. In religion, Zingis established universal toleration. His subjects were idolaters, Jews, Christians, Buddhists and Mahometans.

7. The rich and defenceless empire of China was the first that drew upon itself the hostilities of Zingis. He invaded the northern part of this empire, captured ninety cities, burnt a vast number of towns and villages, and massacred thousands of people. Zingis then turned his arms toward the west, devastating everything in his way.

8. His immense hordes of cavalry swept almost across the entire breadth of the known world, till they reached the eastern portion of Germany. Zingis himself died on the shores of the Caspian Sea, in 1227, as he was on his march to China, to complete the conquest and devastation of that country.

CHAPTER LI.

THE POPE'S EMBASSY TO THE TARTARS.

1. The successors of Zingis Khan pursued his career of conquest. They overran Russia, Poland, Hungary, and still directed their march westward. Europe was struck with inexpressible terror at this new enemy, thrown out, as it were, from the depths of an unknown world. Their immense numbers, and the rapidity of their movements, rendered it vain to fly or to resist.

2. The countries swept by this destroying army were converted at once from the fair abodes of man to smoking deserts. The Tartars were met in Europe by the Duke of Silesia, but that unfortunate prince and his whole army, after a gallant resistance, were put to the sword. The Tartars, however, were somewhat surprised at the courage and resolution shown by the chivalry of Europe.

---

6. What is said of religion? 7. What was done by Zingis in China? 8. What is said of the conquests and death of Zingis?
Chapter LI.—*Questions.*—1. What was done by the successors of Zingis? What by the Duke of Silesia?

3. When they heard, therefore, that the king of Bohemia, the Patriarch of Aquileia, the Duke of Carinthia and other chiefs were approaching with a mighty army, they were seized with apprehension, and withdrew from Europe as speedily as they had advanced. They departed, however, with terrible threats of a quick return; and the people of Europe remained in constant fear, for these new enemies moved with such unparalleled swiftness, that hardly a day's warning could be obtained of their approach.

4. In this crisis, the Pope, or the spiritual ruler of Europe, felt himself called upon to make some effort to deliver the Christian world from so tremendous a scourge. He therefore sent, as ambassadors to the Tartars, two bodies of friars; the one under the direction of Father Ascelin, and the other under that of Father Carpini.

5. These ambassadors were persons taken out of convents, knowing nothing of the common business of life, or of the mode of dealing with mankind. Their only qualification was an awful and unbounded veneration for the pope.

6. Ascelin and his companions found the Tartar army encamped on the northern frontier of Persia. They entered the camp without any ceremony, and being introduced to the Tartar commander, they began by exhorting him to repent of his wickedness, and cease to destroy the Christians. This was listened to by the Tartars without any comment, and the friars were informed that they might have an interview with the khan.

---

3. Why did the Tartars retreat from Europe? 4. What was done by the Pope? 5. What was the character of his ambassadors? 6. What was their conduct in the Tartar camp?

CHAPTER LII.

PERILOUS CONDITION OF THE FRIARS IN THE TARTAR CAMP.

Tartars compelling Ambassadors from the Pope to walk between two fires.

1. While the friars were making preparations for the interview, they learned that they were expected to conform to the custom of the Tartars, by which all who approached the khan, or any of his deputies, were required to kneel three times before him.

2. The friars refused to perform such an act of homage to a heathen; but they informed the Tartars that if they and their prince would become Christians, they would perform the required genuflexions for the honor of the church. At this rash proposition, the rage of the Tartars, which had hitherto been concealed under a veil of politeness, burst all bounds.

Chapter LII.—*Questions.*—1. What ceremony was required of the ambassadors? 2. What answer was made by the friars?

3. They replied that they should be sorry indeed to make themselves Christian dogs like the friars, and they froze the astonished fathers with horror by adding that the Pope was a dog! Ascelin, attempting to reply to these invectives, was silenced by loud cries and menaces.

4. The Tartars immediately held a council to determine what to do with the ambassadors. Some were of opinion that they should be flayed alive, and that their skins, stuffed with hay, should be sent back to the Pope. Others suggested that they might be kept till the next battle with the Christians, and placed in front of it, so as to fall by the hands of their own countrymen.

5. A third advised that they should be whipped through the camp, and then put to death. The Tartar chief, named Baiothnoy, resolved upon their immediate execution, and orders were given to that effect. In this fearful extremity, the lives of the Christian ambassadors were saved by the interposition of a generous female. The principal wife of Baiothnoy, hearing of the fate which impended over these unhappy strangers, ran to her husband to intercede for their lives.

6. Finding him inaccessible to pity, she endeavored to influence him by motives of interest. She represented the disgrace he would incur by violating the law of nations, and reminded him that many ambassadors who now resorted to him with homage and presents, would be deterred from coming.

7. She reminded him also of the deep displeasure expressed by the khan, at his treatment of a former ambassador, whose heart he had caused to be plucked out, and dragged round the camp at the tail of his horse. By these arguments, added to earnest entreaty, she at length obtained his consent to spare the lives of the friars.

---

3. How did the Tartars receive this? 4. What did they propose to do with the friars? 5. What was done by Baiothnoy? 6. What by his wife? 7. How did she remonstrate with her husband? What was her success?

CHAPTER LIII.

END OF FATHER ASCELIN'S EMBASSY.

1. But, although their lives were spared, the ambassadors found their condition very uncomfortable. The Tartars treated them more like cattle than men, and seemed to take delight in harassing and annoying them. They gave them no provisions but black bread and sour milk, and these in so small quantities that they were kept in a state not far from starvation.

2. The Tartar prince often amused himself by sending for them early in the morning, as if to grant them an immediate audience. They were, however, kept the whole day at the outside of his tent, without any shelter, scorched by the rays of a tropical sun, till night, when they were glad to return home, dinnerless and supperless.

3. The Tartars took especial delight in taunting them on the subject of the Pope, a matter respecting which they were peculiarly sensitive. They asked how many armies this prince maintained, and what was the strength of each army; how many battles he had gained; how many kingdoms he had conquered; and finally, whether he had any kingdom at all. The poor friars could return no satisfactory answer to any one of their questions, nor could they give the barbarous Tartars any clear notion of the authority and power of his Holiness of Rome.

4. At this, the Tartars indignantly asked how they could presume to compare so insignificant a personage to the great khan, who had subdued kingdoms innumerable, and who was obeyed by the remotest extremities of the East and West?

5. The unfortunate friars were detained for several months at the Tartar camp, daily but vainly imploring

---

Chapter LIII. — *Questions.* — 1. What was the condition of the friars in the Tartar camp? 2. How did the Tartar prince amuse himself? 3. How did the Tartars annoy the friars? 4. What did they say of the great khan? 5. How did they treat the friars?

their dismissal. The khan, in the mean time, caused every sort of insult to be heaped upon them, and repeatedly showed a disposition to put them to death. These severities he justified by alleging the rude answers which they returned to every question that was put to them.

6. At length the friars obtained their dismissal, with a letter from Baiothnoy to the Pope in the following terms: "Know, Pope, that your messengers have come to us with your letters, and have talked to us in the strangest manner that we ever witnessed. We know not whether you ordered them to do this, but we inform you, that if you wish to keep your seat in Rome, you, Pope, must come to us in your proper person, and do homage to him who commands the whole earth." With this rude epistle, the friars were glad to return from their unfortunate expedition.

CHAPTER LIV.

ADVENTURES OF FATHER CARPINI—HIS DESCRIPTION OF THE TARTARS.

1. In the mean time, Father Carpini, with the other company of friars, were proceeding on their embassy to another horde of Tartars in the north of Europe. They travelled two or three months, when they reached the encampment of a chief named Bathy, who was second in command under the khan, and exercised uncontrolled dominion over all this part of the Tartar world.

2. This place was on the banks of the Volga. The Tartars kindled two great fires, and informed the ambassadors that they must pass through them to purify them from all suspicion of evil. With this strange ceremony they were obliged to comply. The Tartars then provided horses to convey them to the interior of Tartary, where the khan held his court.

---

6. What letter did Baiothnoy write to the Pope? What was the result of the embassy?

CHAPTER LIV.—*Questions.*—1. What is said of Carpini and his companions? 2. How were they received by the Tartars on the Volga?

HIS DESCRIPTION OF THE TARTARS.

3. They travelled through a wide extent of country which had recently been ravaged by the Tartars, and for many days saw the melancholy spectacle of human skulls and bones strewed everywhere in their route. At length they reached the court of the khan, where they passed some months in vain endeavors to negotiate with this monarch.

4. Carpini brought to Europe the first precise description of these terrible warriors whose name had struck a terror into all Christendom. "They are broad," says he, "between the eyes and the balls of the cheeks; they have little flat noses, small eyes, and eyelids standing straight upright. They are shaven on the crown, like priests."

5. He also relates some very marvellous stories of the wars and invasions of the Tartars. According to these accounts, when the invaders approached Mount Caucasus, they met with a mountain of adamant, which drew into it all the arrows and darts of iron which were discharged in its neighborhood. When they attempted to penetrate this mountain, they encountered a huge black cloud which completely obstructed their passage.

6. This seems to be an exaggerated statement of the simple fact, that the Tartar army, accustomed only to the dead level of their vast plains, were unable to contend with an enemy amid the rocks and defiles of this vast chain of mountains. The Tartars also related, that in a country lying on the ocean, they found monsters with men's heads but dogs' faces, who spoke two words like men, but at the third barked like dogs.

7. Another country is described where the men were of the human shape, but the women were shaped like dogs. These latter rubbed themselves in the snow till it froze round them in a solid mass, and formed a complete armor, from which the arrows of the Tartars rebounded as if they had struck upon iron.

8. This fabulous tale indicates an acquaintance with the shores of the Eastern Ocean and the dogs of the

---

3. What did the ambassadors witness on their travels? 4. How does Carpini describe the Tartars? 5. What stories does he tell of them? 6. What explanation is given? What country was described by the Tartars? 7. What description did they give of a certain people? 8. How is this explained?

Kamtschadales. These frozen regions had evidently checked the invasions of the Tartars in the east.

9. On their march toward Armenia, they are said to have met a tribe of people, each individual of which had only one arm and one leg, so that it required two of them to draw a bow. These persons are described as running with incredible swiftness, sometimes hopping on their single foot, and sometimes with hand and foot together.

10. Another country was said to be so near the rising of the sun, that the inhabitants could not endure the terrible noise which he made on rising, and always stopped their ears at daybreak!

11. Carpini describes a country in India where the people had images of copper with fire in them, which they placed on horseback, while a man with a pair of bellows rode behind. When the horses were drawn up in battle array, the men laid something on the fire within the images and blew strongly with the bellows. "Whereupon, it came to pass," says he, " that the men and the horses were burnt with wild fire, and the air was darkened with smoke." From this account, it is supposed that gunpowder had been invented, and was in use in Asia at a time when it was unknown in Europe.

12. The embassy of Carpini to the Tartars proved as fruitless as that of Ascelin. The friars returned to Rome in safety, after a journey of unparalleled dangers and hardships, and were rejoiced over by their friends " as men that had risen from death unto life." These events took place about 1250 A. D.

---

9. What is said of a tribe of people near Armenia? 10. What of a country near the rising sun? 11. What of a country in India? 12. What was the result of the embassy of Carpini?

CHAPTER LV.

THE TARTAR DOMINION.

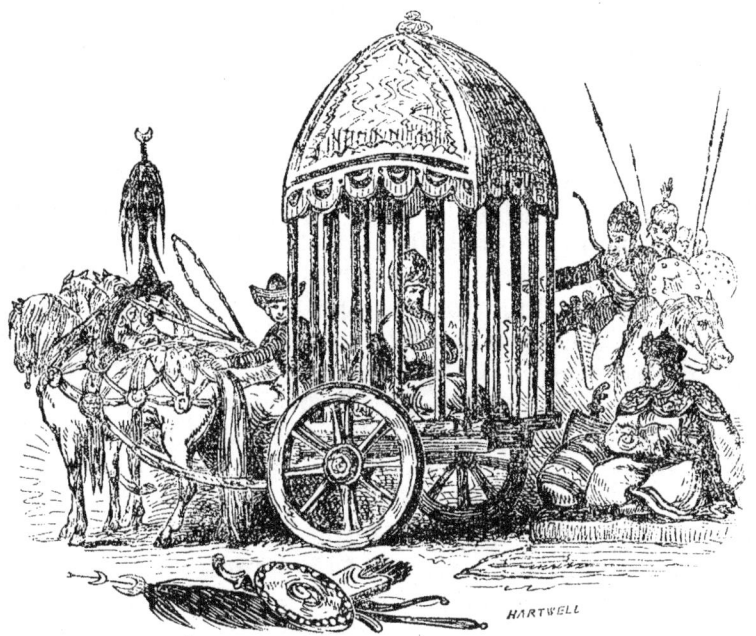

Bajazet in a cage before Tamerlane.

1. The successors of Zingis Khan became the sovereigns of almost all Asia. But this great empire was soon divided. In the 14th century arose Timour or Tamerlane, who distinguished himself by his conquests. He defeated Bajazet, the Turkish sultan, took him prisoner, and shut him up in an iron cage. This victory crushed, for a time, the rising power of the Ottoman empire.

2. Timour invaded Hindostan and seized the throne of that country, where a branch of his family continued to reign for 500 years afterwards. These sovereigns were called the *Mogul Emperors*. In China, the Tartar power continued to hold the sway long after it had declined in other quarters. But at length the Chinese expelled these foreigners, and placed a native prince on

---

Chapter LV.—*Questions.*—1. What is said of Timour? 2. His invasion of Hindostan? What took place in China?

the throne. This change of dynasty, however, was not permanent.

3. In the 17th century, the Mantchoos, a race of eastern Tartars, reduced China once more to subjection. To this empire they subsequently added not only the conquering state of Mantchoo Tartary, but the whole of the Mongolian territory. as far as the frontier of Asiatic Russia. Over all this region the Chinese government has established a very mild dominion, leaving the internal administration of affairs almost wholly in the hands of the natives.

4. The Mongols and the Turks are the two leading races among the various tribes which inhabit the immense regions known under the general name of Tartary. The Mongols now occupy the pastoral districts bounded on the north by the great Desert of Shamo.

5. The personal aspect of the Mongols is strange and almost deformed. Their faces are broad, flat and square, with high cheek-bones, a flat nose, small and sharp black eyes, set obliquely, thick lips, and scanty black hair. The Calmucks, the Kalkas, the Eluths and the Burats, are branches of the great Mongol family.

6. The Turks are a much handsomer race, having none of the Mongol deformities, but clear, ruddy complexions. The present tribes in Tartary are divided, chiefly, into the Uzbeks, the Turkomans, and the Kuznauks. The Mantchoos have the Mongol features, with a fairer complexion; they are considered as of the Mongol stock.

7. Although this great variety exists in the external appearance of these races, yet they all agree, to a certain extent, in manners and mode of life. The same wandering, pastoral, equestrian habits, the same division into tribes, the same absolute sway of their khans, unite in fixing a similar character on all the nations which bear the name of Tartar.

8. Among some of the tribes, many customs, similar to those of our Indians, are found, leading to the belief that the latter derived their ancestry from Tartary.

---

3. What is said of the Mantchoos? 4. Of the Mongols and Turks? 5. What is the personal appearance of the Mongols? 6. What of the Turks? 7. In what respect do these different races resemble each other? 8. What of the American Indians?

CHINA.

CHAPTER LVI.

ANCIENT HISTORY OF CHINA.

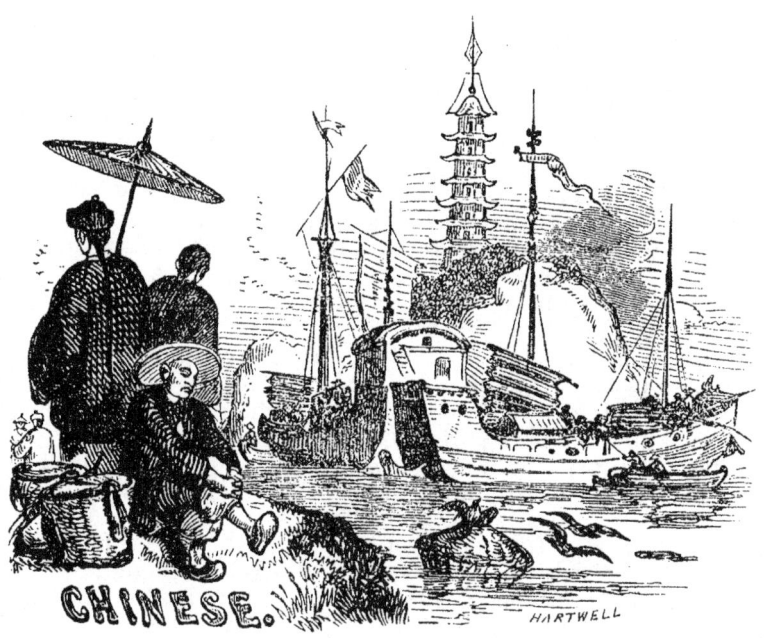

1. CHINA* is a very large country, in the eastern part of Asia. On the north, a stupendous wall, 1250 miles

---

* China is remarkable as being the most populous empire in the world. It embraces China Proper, Corea, Chinese Tartary and Thibet. It is therefore not only the most populous, but the most extensive empire in the world, except Russia. China has long excited the curiosity and interest of the world, from its great antiquity, its immense population, its exclusion of foreigners, and its jealous policy. The country is an immense plain, the climate being as cold as in America, in the same latitudes.

The Great Wall, built two thousand years ago, as a defence against the Tartars, is twelve hundred and fifty miles long, and employed several millions of men five years for its construction.

CHAPTER LVI.—*Questions.*—1. Describe China.

in length, separates it from the deserts of Tartary. The sea washes its coast on the south-east. The kingdoms of Chin India, or Farther India, border it on the south-west, and on the west it is separated from Thibet by lofty mountains.

2. The face of the country is exceedingly varied: an immense tract of it is occupied by mountains and valleys. Rivers are numerous; and two of them, the Hoang-ho and the Yang-tse-Kiang, are among the largest

This, with the Imperial Canal, from Pekin to Nankin, six hundred miles long, evinces the patient energy of the emperors and the people. The government is a despotism. The emperor claims to rule by the appointment of Heaven; and, while his titles are lofty, he displays a benignant and patriarchal spirit toward the people. The officers of government are called mandarins.

Pekin, the capital, is one of the largest cities in the world. Nankin, the ancient capital, has decayed from its former splendor. Canton is the commercial emporium, and, till recently, the only place where Europeans and Americans were permitted to trade. Macao, on an island in the Canton River, belongs to the Portuguese, and is the residence of the families of the Europeans who have business at Canton. The women of China are kept as closely as those of Turkey. Those of the wealthy class have their feet bandaged, so that when grown, they are but four inches long. The rich have generally several wives.

Chinese Tartary comprises several distinct branches of the Tartar family. These are the Mantchoos, Mongolians, Soongarians, &c. They possess the general Tartar characteristics already described. Most of them are worshippers of the Grand Lama.

Thibet is the seat of the worship of the Grand Lama. This is a lofty region, embracing the sublime peaks of Chumularee, the highest mountain in the world. Lassa is the capital, and here is the temple of the Grand Lama. This exalted being is some one selected by the priests, into whose soul the spirit of the preceding Lama is said to have passed. He is deemed the representative of Buddha, or God on earth, and is worshipped with the most profound adoration. His temple is said to contain ten thousand rooms. It has towers and obelisks covered with gold and silver, and a multitude of images, of the same precious metals. The Thibetians are a pastoral people, and rear the mountain goat, whose hair, or wool, is so much valued for the manufacture of shawls. Here also is the *yak*, a peculiar species of ox, whose tail is terminated with long silky hair.

Corea is a large peninsula, the people resembling those of China. Little is known of this country. The inhabitants are said to be great thieves, and if a sailor is shipwrecked on the coast, he is reduced to slavery.

2. Its rivers, soil, &c.

ANCIENT HISTORY OF CHINA.

in the world. A great part of the soil is fertile, and every spot susceptible of tillage is cultivated in the most careful and industrious manner.

3. The Chinese call their country *Choong Kwo*, or the Middle Kingdom, because they formerly imagined that it was situated in the centre of the earth, and that all other countries lay scattered around their empire in the form of small islands.

4. In later times, they have, indeed, more correct notions of geography; but so pertinaciously do they adhere to ancient opinions, and especially to whatever flatters their national vanity, that they still persist in expressing themselves in this absurd manner.

5. The early history of China is fabulous, like that of almost every other ancient nation; but the Chinese historical fables are extravagant in an uncommon degree. Puan-koo, the first monarch or legislator of this country, is said to have worn a dress of leaves. All the stories concerning him are very wild and obscure.

6. After Puan-koo came other monarchs, who reigned many thousands of years, till the appearance of Fo-hi, who invented music and arithmetic, and brought his subjects from barbarism to civilization. Little dependence, however, can be placed on Chinese history previous to the time of Confucius, who lived about 500 years before Christ.

7. At the time of the birth of Confucius, China was divided into a number of independent states, which were almost constantly at war with each other. His earliest efforts as a reformer were exerted to unite them in one great confederation.

8. Confucius made a collection of the old traditions of the country, and drew from them a body of moral lessons and political maxims designed to form the basis of good government. The main principle of his system was, that outward decorum of behavior is the test and emblem of moral goodness; he also insisted that reverence to parents and grand-parents was a primary virtue.

3, 4. What do the Chinese call their country, and what idea have they of its situation? 5. What is said of the early history of China? 6. What of Puan-koo? 7. What was the state of China at the birth of Confucius? 8. What work was compiled by Confucius, and what did he teach?

9. On these foundations he constructed a ritual or political guide-book, in which every relation of public and private life was illustrated by rules and precepts, and the duties and manners of every citizen were properly defined. This work was gradually received as a standard authority by the nation, and retains its influence among the Chinese to the present day.

CHAPTER LVII.

TARTAR CONQUEST OF CHINA.

Chinese emperor ordering the books to be burned.

1. ALL China appears to have been first united under one sovereign by Chin-Wang, otherwise called Chi Hoang Ti. He was the founder of the Tsin dynasty, and flourished about two centuries and a half before

---

9. How did the Chinese receive his teachings?

CHAPTER LVII.—*Questions.*—1. When and by whom was China united under one sovereign?

Christ. This is the sovereign who is said to have built the great wall, to defend his empire from the incursions of the northern Tartars.

2. This famous structure remains at the present day, though parts of it are in a state of decay; it is one of the most remarkable monuments of human industry on the face of the globe. It passes over high mountains, and crosses deep valleys. In many places it is very strongly built, and fortified with towers at regular intervals. It is for the most part of brick, resting on foundations of stone.

3. Chin-Wang also attempted to destroy all the literature of China, hoping to extinguish the remembrance of the sovereigns who had reigned before him. For this purpose, he ordered all the books of the learned, including those of Confucius, to be thrown into the fire. But, notwithstanding this order, many of the books were preserved.

4. Under the dynasty of Han, which arose shortly after this, literature was zealously cultivated; printing was invented, and the laws were collected into a regular system. For these reasons, the Han dynasty is accounted one of the most glorious in the Chinese annals.

5. In the 13th century after Christ, the Tartars, under Zingis Khan, invaded China and conquered a great part of the country. Kublai Khan, his grandson, completed the work. During the war, the young son of the Chinese emperor fled to the sea-coast and took refuge on board the fleet. The Tartar ships attacked them, and after an engagement which lasted a whole day, the Chinese admiral saw that escape was impossible.

6. He went to the prince, who stood on the deck, and said, "It is better to die free than to dishonor our ancestors by an inglorious captivity." Then, without waiting for a reply, he caught the prince in his arms and sprang into the sea, where they both perished. In this manner China was subjugated by the Tartars or Mongols.

7. Kublai Khan, or Shee-Tsoo, as he is called in the Chinese histories, governed the conquered people with

---

2. Describe the great wall. 3. What is said of the burning of the books? 4. What of the dynasty of Han? 5. What of Zingis and Kublai Khan? 6. What is said of the death of a Chinese prince? 7. Of the reign of Kublai Khan?

wisdom and mildness. He adhered as closely as possible to the ancient laws and customs of the empire, patronized learned men, and honored the memory of Confucius.

8. By these means he reconciled the Chinese to his government. He also constructed the great canal, which, with various branches, is of vast extent. This immense work is not only one of the wonders of the world, but it is one of the greatest benefits ever conferred on the Chinese empire.

CHAPTER LVIII.

CONQUEST OF CHINA BY THE MANTCHOOS.

The Chinese submitting to Chun Tchi.

1. THE Mongols retained possession of the throne of China upwards of a hundred years. They administered

---

8. The grand canal?
CHAPTER LVIII.—*Questions.*—1. What is said of the Mongols in China?

the government wisely, and labored to extend the foreign commerce of the nation. But on the failure of the direct royal line, the Mongols became involved in a civil war for the succession to the throne. This so weakened them that the Chinese were tempted to rise in insurrection.

2. The son of a poor laborer, named Choo Quen Tchang, put himself at the head of the insurgents, and in a war of a few months, drove the Mongols beyond the great wall. This successful warrior was elevated to the throne, and became the founder of the Ming dynasty. This race of princes maintained the throne till nearly the middle of the seventeenth century.

3. They were succeeded by the Mantchoo Tartars, who invaded China from the northern deserts, and taking advantage of the civil discords which then prevailed in the empire, gained possession of the capital and established their authority there. For many years, the Chinese in the other quarters of the empire, continued to resist the invaders; but after the whole country had been ravaged by hostilities, the inhabitants submitted, and the Mantchoo Tartar power was fully established in China, A. D. 1644.

4. Chun Tchi, the first emperor of this dynasty, governed the conquered empire with wisdom and moderation. He adopted the Chinese method of appointing no man to office without making a strict inquiry as to his talents and fitness. To secure the influence of the Tartars without degrading his conquered subjects, he composed the tribunals of justice and administration by taking half the members from each nation.

5. Kang Hi, the son of this emperor, succeeded to the throne at the age of eight years. The talents which he displayed during his long reign of 61 years, caused him to be ranked among the most illustrious of the Chinese sovereigns. To his wisdom are owing the unity and domestic peace which the empire has enjoyed from his accession down to the present day.

6. He made great exertions to introduce the arts and

---

2. Of the foundation of the Ming dynasty? 3. Of the Mantchoo Tartars? 4. Of the reign of Chun Tchi? 5. Of Kang Hi? 6. Of the Jesuits in China?

sciences of Europe into China. He patronized the Jesuit missionaries who resorted to his court, and profited so much by their instructions as to learn geometry, on which science the emperor himself wrote an able treatise. The learned men of China, however, set themselves with bigoted obstinacy against the introduction of foreign learning.

7. The efforts of Kang Hi to give a new tone to Chinese literature were, in a great measure, frustrated. He died in 1722, and was succeeded by his son Yung Tching, who did not attempt to pursue his father's enlightened policy. In his reign, the Catholic missionaries had spread themselves all over China and made many converts.

8. The Jesuits, who were the leaders in this undertaking, gave great alarm to the government, by their extravagant doctrines respecting the supremacy of the Pope, in consequence of which they were all banished from the empire, with the exception of a few whom the emperor chose to keep near his court, where he found them useful in matters of science and literature. A considerable number of Catholic missionaries have continued in China to the present time.

CHAPTER LIX.

REIGN OF KIEN LONG—THE CHINESE PIRATES.

1. YUNG TCHING, nevertheless, is allowed, even by the missionaries, to have had some good qualities. He seems to have felt a strong attachment to the early institutions of China, and the maxims of her ancient sages. He revived many antique usages which had fallen into neglect, particularly the festivals in honor of virtue, the observances of filial piety, and the honor rendered to agriculture by the emperor, who, once in the year, held the plough with his own hand.

2. After a reign of thirteen years, he was succeeded,

---

7. Of Yung Tching? 8. What became of the Jesuits?
CHAPTER LIX.—*Questions.*—1. How did Yung Tching reign?

REIGN OF KIEN LONG.

in 1736, by Tchien Lung, more commonly called Kien Long. This prince displayed a mild and intelligent character, and not only gave great encouragement to literature, but excelled in authorship himself. He showed a strong disposition to relax the severities against the Christians, and it was only by means of the urgent representations of the mandarins and tribunals that he was induced to treat them with rigor.

3. His generals carried on war with the tribes on the western frontiers of the empire, and reduced Thibet to the Chinese dominion. The fame of Kien Long extended to Europe, and embassies from Holland, Great Britain and Russia were sent to his court, with a view to establish commercial intercourse with China. These attempts, however, were not followed by the expected results.

4. The Chinese believed themselves the only enlightened nation in the universe, and claimed homage from all others as barbarians. The emperor himself appears to have been free from these prejudices, but all the officers of state opposed any increase of foreign intercourse, which they feared would in some way be injurious.

5. In 1795, Kien Long, having reached the age of 85, abdicated, and was succeeded by his son, Kia King. This prince was naturally of a good disposition; but after his accession to the throne he sunk into indolent and luxurious habits, which lowered his character in the eyes of his subjects. The spirit of disaffection which had begun to appear under his predecessor now assumed a serious aspect.

6. The empire was no longer disturbed, as in ancient times, by the ambition of governors, but there had arisen among the people a number of brotherhoods or associations, which endeavored to control or subvert the government. The most formidable of these bodies assumed the name of the *White Water Flower*, and excited a formidable insurrection, which was not quelled

---

2. What was the character of Kien Long? 3. What is said of his wars and intercourse with foreign nations? 4. What of Chinese prejudices? 5. What was the character of Kia King? 6. What insurrections took place in his reign?

till it had kept the empire in a state of disturbance for eight years. Another of these associations took the name of the *Votaries of Celestial Reason.* They captured the imperial palace at Pekin, and kept possession of it for several days, but at length they were defeated.

7. In this reign, also, piracy was practised to a most formidable extent along the coast of China. The pirates were estimated at 70,000 men, and their vessels at 1800. Their leader, Ching Yih, was accidentally drowned, but his widow assumed the command with a true Amazonian spirit.

8. She led on the fleets to battle, and administered the affairs of the piratical confederacy with the greatest vigor. She made a code of laws, by which these fierce rovers were controlled and obliged to observe the rules of equity towards each other. She imposed a regular tax on the merchant shipping, upon payment of which she granted passes; without these no vessel could safely navigate the Chinese seas.

9. This singular female long bade defiance to the whole maritime force of the empire, but her power was at length weakened by factions among her followers, and they finally abandoned their piracy and entered the imperial service.

CHAPTER LX.

RECENT TRANSACTIONS IN CHINA.

1. Kia King died in 1820, and was succeeded by Taou Kwang, the present emperor. He is favorably spoken of by those who have enjoyed opportunities of knowing him. In the early part of his reign, a wild tribe of mountaineers in the south, called Dog-men, rose in rebellion, and caused great alarm at court. Their leader took the title of sovereign, and threatened to

---

7. What is said of piracy? 8. How were the pirates governed? 9. What became of them?

Chapter LX.—*Questions.*—1. What is the character of Taou Kwang? What is said of the Dog-men?

march upon Pekin, but the movement was frustrated by his sudden death.

2. A rebellion also took place in the island of Formosa, which was not suppressed till 1833. The portion of Bokhara which had been conquered by Kien Long, was likewise disturbed by insurrections, occasioned by the interdiction of the exportation of tea and rhubarb, and the rebels maintained their ground for several years. It is said that many parts of the interior are still in a state of hostility with the imperial government.

3. The most serious affair in which the Chinese have been involved during the present century, was that of the war with Great Britain. This was occasioned by the following circumstances. The Chinese have been for many years addicted to smoking opium, a practice which is pursued for the purpose of intoxication. The government, with a view of checking this pernicious habit, prohibited the importation of opium into the empire.

4. The passion for this drug, however, had become so strong and universal among all ranks of people, that vast quantities of it continued to be smuggled into the country. At length, the government seized several cargoes of opium belonging to British merchants, and destroyed it.

5. The British demanded payment, but were refused. A British fleet was immediately despatched to China, to compel the government to make restitution. Canton was bombarded, and Nankin and several other places captured by the British forces. Although the Chinese mustered very large armies, yet the superiority of their numbers availed nothing against the superior weapons, the courage, skill and discipline of the British.

6. The court at length judged it prudent to submit to the demands of the invaders, and a treaty was signed, by which six millions of dollars were paid by the Emperor as an indemnity for the opium destroyed. The

---

2. Of the rebellion in Bokhara? 3, 4. How did the opium war with the British originate? 5. What was the success of the British? 6. What treaty was made between Great Britain and China?

emperor also ceded to the British the island of Hong Kong, and opened the ports of Amoy, Foutchow, Ningpo and Shanghae, including Canton, to the trade of foreign nations. These events took place in 1840 and the two succeeding years.

7. Three years afterwards, the United States sent a commissioner to China, who negotiated a treaty for the promotion of American commerce, and intercourse with the empire and the security of our citizens in that country. These transactions, it is thought, will have great effect in making the Chinese government and people better acquainted with Europeans and Americans, and gradually remove the unsocial feeling and exclusive spirit which have hitherto characterized their intercourse with foreign nations.

8. Already the Chinese begin to show signs of enterprise, before unknown. Several of their vessels have lately arrived at California, and a number of the people are settled in that country. The emperor Taou Kwang, died in 1850.

CHAPTER LXI.

POPULATION, MANNERS, ETC., OF THE CHINESE.

1. CHINA is the most populous empire in the world. As we have said, it contains three hundred millions of inhabitants. The large cities are so full of people, that great numbers live in boats on the rivers and canals. The Chinese are very industrious, and cultivate the soil with great care. Every part of the country is laid out in fields, gardens and pastures. The chief food of the inhabitants is rice, but almost everything produced by the soil is eaten. They also eat many animals which other nations regard as unfit for food, as dogs, cats, &c.

2. The most celebrated of all the native productions of China is tea, an article which is not raised in full perfection in any other part of the world. The tea-plant

---

7. What between the United States and China? 8. What of California?

CHAPTER LXI.—*Questions.*—1. What is said of the population of China? Industry, agriculture, food, &c.? 2. Of the cultivation of tea?

is a shrub five or six feet in height. The leaves of this are dried in different ways, and according to the different seasons at which they are gathered, and the nature of the soil on which they grow, the different qualities of tea are produced.

3. Silk is another article for which the world was originally indebted to China, and it has been manufactured in that country for more than 2000 years. The Chinese were the first inventors of paper, the mariner's compass, gunpowder, printing, fire-works, and many other things now common in all civilized nations.

4. The better classes of the Chinese dress in long and loose garments of silk; they esteem tight dresses, like those of the Europeans, highly unbecoming. They shave their hair, except a tuft on the crown, which they plait into a long queue like a whip-lash, extending sometimes below the knees. They wear peaked hats, and both men and women carry fans.

5. People of fashion suffer their finger-nails to grow to an enormous length, and to guard them from accident, they cover them with sheaths of bamboo. They regard small feet as a very great beauty in a woman, and for this reason they swathe up tightly the feet of their female children, so that they cease to grow. A Chinese lady of high breeding is therefore scarcely able to walk on account of the smallness of her feet. The lower classes, however, cannot afford to mutilate the feet of their females, but make a natural use of them like the Europeans.

6. China abounds with large and populous cities. Pekin, the capital, is thought to contain two millions of inhabitants. It is very regularly built, in squares, and is surrounded with walls fifty feet high, and so thick that horsemen gallop along the top without danger. Nankin and Canton are also very large cities. The latter is a seaport, and has an active commerce: nearly all the European trade with China is carried on at this place.

7. The government of China, like that of most Asiatic nations, is very arbitrary. The emperor is called the

---

3. Of silk, paper, gunpowder, &c.? 4. How do the Chinese dress? 5. What singular customs have they? 6. What is said of their cities? 7. What is the nature of their government?

Son of Heaven. The Chinese speak of foreigners with great contempt, calling them "outside barbarians," "black devils," and other opprobrious names. The chief religion of China is Buddhism, or the doctrine of Fo; there are many idols in the temples, which the common people worship. The more learned bestow divine honors upon Confucius, the great philosopher and moralist of China.

THIBET.

CHAPTER LXII.

HISTORICAL SKETCH—THE GRAND LAMA.

The Grand Lama.

1. THIBET is the most southern of the three great table-lands of Central Asia. It is bounded on the north by the great desert of Tartary; on the east by China;

How do they speak of foreigners?
CHAPTER LXII.—*Questions.*—1. Describe Thibet.

on the south by Hindostan, Assam and Burmah; and on the west by Hindostan and Tartary.

2. Little is known of the geography of the country, except that it is very lofty and mountainous. The Hindoos and Chinese call it the land of hunger and misery. There are, however, in Thibet many fertile valleys, where the climate is comparatively mild.

3. According to the traditions of the inhabitants this country was originally inhabited by brute animals and demons. At a certain period, the king of the monkeys came to Thibet and led the life of a hermit, performing religious duties and studying the sublime science of *nothing*.

4. Just as he was on the point of gaining a full knowledge of this subject, he was disturbed in his contemplations by a female *Mangus* or ugly demon, who had assumed a beautiful figure, and proposed to the monkey-king that they should be married. The wedding took place, and the descendants of this lovely pair are the present inhabitants of Thibet.

5. Absurd and puerile as this story is, it is a sacred and important thing in the estimation of the Thibetians, who believe in the transmigration of souls, and are proud of their descent from a monkey, because he is one of the most cunning of animals.

6. The first accounts of the real history of Thibet are in the annals of the Mongols and Chinese. The Thibetians seem to belong to the Mongolian race. They were at first divided into many independent tribes which led a nomadic life.

7. Of the first king of Thibet, a story is related similar to that of the birth of Moses: He was exposed by his father, and found swimming in a copper box on the Ganges. He became king B. C. 313. It appears that Buddhism was introduced into this country about the middle of the 5th century after Christ.

8. In the time of Strongdsar Gambo, who reigned in

---

2. What is known of it? 3. What traditions have the inhabitants? 4. What is said of a monkey-wedding? 5. What religious belief have the Thibetians? 6. What is the early history of Thibet? 7. What story is told of the first king of Thibet? When was Buddhism introduced into the country? 8. What is said of the Thibetian alphabet?

the 7th century, Tongmi Samsoda is said to have invented the Thibetian alphabet, which is a modification of the Sanscrit. Mahometanism was introduced in the century following, but Buddhism regained the ascendency in the 16th century.

9. The Thibetians were for a long period an independent people, though their country was many times invaded and plundered by the Tartars. Towards the end of the last century the king of the neighboring territory of Nepaul overran Thibet with his armies, and put the country under tribute. The emperor of China interfered by sending 70,000 men, who expelled the Nepaul armies and established his own authority in Thibet.

10. This country is at present a province of China, but is governed with mildness by its conquerors. The ancient forms of administration are allowed to remain. The Grand Lama is nominally the chief magistrate, but the affairs of government are mainly conducted by the agents of the Chinese emperor. The Grand Lama is the spiritual head of the Buddhist religion, as the Pope is the head of the Catholic church in general.

11. The Grand Lama lives at Pootala, seven miles east of Lassa, the capital of Thibet. His temple is three hundred and seventy feet high, filled with images of gold and silver, and decorated on the outside in a costly manner. Numerous priests and monks are in constant attendance. Travellers who have visited China and Thibet, say that the worship of the Grand Lama greatly resembles the worship in Catholic churches.

12. When a Grand Lama dies, the priests select another, very much as the cardinals of Europe select a new pope, when the old one is dead. The Lama pretends to be God himself, and the priests make the people believe that he is so.

13. The Grand Lama is only to be seen in the remote parts of his palace. Here he is found, seeming to be in a profound reverie. Thousands of people come and bring him rich presents; and they think themselves well paid, if he lays his hand upon their heads.

---

9. Of the political revolutions of Thibet? 10. What is the present condition and government of this country? 11. What of the Grand Lama and his temple? 12. What of the Grand Lama and the Pope? 13. How is the Grand Lama seen?

JAPAN.

CHAPTER LXIII.

ANCIENT HISTORY OF THE JAPANESE EMPIRE.

1. The Empire of Japan* comprises a group of islands lying to the east of the Asiatic continent, and

---

* Japan is a populous empire, strongly resembling China in its institutions. It includes Niphon and the adjacent islands. The country is highly cultivated, and many arts are carried to a considerable degree of perfection. The people are polite and ceremonious. A high sense of honor, integrity, and devoted friendship, are characteristics of the people. Education receives great attention, and females are instructed with care.

Buddhism prevails extensively; but a native religion, called Sinto, is the faith of the mass. The Dairi is the spiritual ruler of the country, but the Cubo is the political ruler, paying only nominal obedience to the Dairi. Jeddo, the capital, is one of the great cities of the world. Meaco is the residence of the Dairi,

---

Chapter LXIII.—*Questions.*—1. Describe Japan.

separated from each other by narrow channels. The largest of these islands, named Niphon, is about 800 miles in length.

2. This empire is one of the most populous in the world, considering its extent, and its political and social institutions are marked by such striking and peculiar features, that, notwithstanding its remote and insulated situation, it has justly attracted a large share of the curiosity of Europe and America.

3. Japan was entirely unknown to the ancients. This empire, however, has its records, which pretend to give an account of the revolutions of this country for many thousands of years. Setting aside the evidently fabulous part of this history, the first sovereigns or lawgivers of Japan appear to have come from China, and brought with them the rudiments of civilization.

4. About 600 years before the Christian era, the dynasty of the *Dairis* became established in Japan. These rulers laid claim to a descent from the ancient celestial sovereigns of the country, and called themselves "Sons of Heaven." The dairi was, in fact, a sort of Pope, and exercised both a civil and ecclesiastical authority.

5. These rulers, however, after a sway of many centuries, sunk at length into voluptuous indolence, and devolved the cares of government upon the Cubo Sama, or Ziogoon. This officer, who was at first only general of the armies, contrived to monopolize nearly all the authority of the government; and thus, about the 16th century, a complete revolution was accomplished in the political constitution of the empire.

6. The profound veneration, however, entertained by the nation for the dairi, and the sacred character which he bore, rendered it impossible that his power should be wholly overthrown. He still enjoys ample revenues

---

and chief seat of literature. Nangasaki is the only place Europeans are permitted to visit, the same exclusive policy prevailing here as in China.

---

2. Its population, &c.? 3. What is said of its early history? 4. When was the dynasty of the Daris established? What was the Dairi? 5. What became of his power? What is said of the Ziogoon? 6. What is the present power of the Dairi?

to maintain his dignity, with an absolute control over all spiritual concerns.

7. The intercourse of the Christian nations with Japan is the most interesting portion of its history. The Portuguese first visited these islands about the year 1543. The Japanese did not then exhibit that jealousy of foreigners which marks their conduct at the present day.

8. The Portuguese were received in a friendly manner. They were allowed to establish a factory and carry on a great trade at Firando, and introduced missionaries who preached Christianity among the natives. Francis Xavier, the celebrated Catholic apostle of the East, made Japan the chief theatre of his labors, and such was the zeal of the missionaries, that they succeeded in converting great numbers of the people, among whom were several princes.

CHAPTER LXIV.

THE PORTUGUESE AND DUTCH IN JAPAN.

1. These fair prospects however were soon clouded. The Jesuit missionaries displayed great eagerness not only to make converts, but to obtain the gold of the Japanese. The jealousy of the despotic administration was roused, and very soon the Jesuits were found to be implicated in a conspiracy against the government.

2. This at once excited a violent hostility against the Portuguese and their converts. A general persecution was raised against all, both native and foreign, who professed the new faith, and it was carried on with an unrelenting severity characteristic of the Japanese. The Christians suffered long and with unshaken constancy, but at length they were exterminated or suppressed.

3. The Portuguese were expelled from the empire,

---

7. When did the Portuguese first visit Japan? 8. How were they received?

Chapter LXIV.—*Questions.*—1. What was done by the Jesuits? 2. What was the consequence of this? 3. What is said of the Dutch in Japan?

after numbers of them had been put to death. The Dutch had previously obtained a footing in Japan, and were too cautious and circumspect to hazard their safety by intermeddling with the politics of the Japanese. They were, in consequence, allowed to remain in the country.

4. At the present day the Dutch are the only foreigners, except the Chinese, who are permitted to visit Japan or maintain any commercial intercourse with the inhabitants. They have a trading establishment on a small island in the harbor of Nangasaki, where they are kept in strict seclusion, little better than imprisonment.

5. All attempts made by other Christian nations to obtain an intercourse with Japan have completely failed. When a foreign ship approaches the shore she is ordered away. If by stress of weather or a want of provisions she is compelled to put into a Japanese harbor, she is immediately surrounded by a fleet of guard-boats that her crew may hold no communication with the shore.

6. Provisions and other necessary things are supplied her, free of cost, and she is compelled to depart without delay. Foreigners shipwrecked on the coast of Japan are immediately imprisoned and closely guarded: after being minutely examined and kept in a tedious captivity, which sometimes lasts for years, they are sent to the Dutch at Nangasaki to be shipped out of the empire.

7. The laws of Japan are very severe, and the government is completely despotic. The laws, however, are most strictly observed, and the security of person and property is nowhere better established than in this country.

---

4. What is their condition at present? 5. How are foreign ships treated by the Japanese? 6. How shipwrecked foreigners? 7. What is said of the laws of Japan?

CHAPTER LXV.

COMMERCIAL POLICY OF THE JAPANESE.

1. No Japanese is allowed to leave his native country for the purpose of visiting any other part of the world, this being prohibited under penalty of death. Formerly, the Japanese made long voyages in their own vessels to Corea, China, Java, Formosa, and other places, but the art of navigation has now much declined among them.

2. This, however, does not prevent them from making short voyages along their shores with an immense number of trading vessels and fishing-smacks. They seldom venture so far out to sea as to be in danger of losing sight of land, and always keep in the neighborhood of some secure harbor, in case of a storm.

3. They have a knowledge of the compass, which they probably obtained from the Chinese, but their vessels are ill-adapted to sea navigation, being open at the stern, with very large and clumsy rudders. No vessels are allowed to carry any cannon, or to be painted red, except those of the emperor.

4. Yet the Japanese, if they desired it, might have a very good navy. They need only invite into their country two or three good naval architects and some naval officers. They have good ports, good carpenters, all the necessary materials, and very active and enterprising sailors.

5. The Japanese people are, in general, quick of apprehension and ready at learning. The sailors, trained in the European manner, would soon make their fleets able to contend with those of Europe. The Dutch who have lived at Nangasaki, mention the wonderful activity of the Japanese sailors, and declare that it is hardly credible to see with what dexterity they manage their great boats in the violent surf, and the most rapid currents at the mouths of the rivers.

CHAPTER LXV.—*Questions.*—1. What restrictions are placed upon the Japanese? 2. What commerce have they? 3. What is said of their ships? 4. Their capacities for commerce? 5. What is the general character of the Japanese?

6. These men are well paid for their dangerous and laborious services, but they are, like the English sailors, great spendthrifts, and squander in a few days, in public-houses, the money which it cost them months to gain at the hazard of their lives.

CHAPTER LXVI.

INTERCOURSE OF THE JAPANESE WITH STRANGERS.

1. Although the Japanese have no custom-houses, and impose no duties upon goods either imported or exported, yet the utmost vigilance is exercised to prevent smuggling prohibited commodities into the country. All persons as well as packages which are landed, are subjected to so strict a watching, that the hundred eyes of Argus may be said to be employed in this preventive service of the Japanese government.

2. When any European goes ashore, he is first searched on board the ship, and then a second time as soon as he sets foot on the land. Both examinations are very strict, so that the traveller's pockets are turned inside out, and every part of his dress pulled, pinched and tumbled. Even the hair of the head is sometimes closely searched.

3. All the Japanese that go on board any vessels are likewise subjected to this process, excepting only the superior order of *banjoses*. All articles exported or imported undergo a similar search, and large chests and boxes are so curiously examined, that they sound the boards, suspecting them to be hollow.

4. Beds are ripped open in this search, and the feathers sifted. Iron scoops are thrust into tubs of butter and jars of sweetmeats. Holes are cut in cheeses, so that a mouse could not be smuggled into Japan by hiding

---

6. Of the sailors?
Chapter LXVI.—*Questions.*—1. What is said of smuggling in Japan? 2. How are Europeans searched? 3. How the Japanese? 4. How other things?

himself inside. And what seems carrying the matter to a most ridiculous excess, they sometimes break open the eggs which the Dutch carry from Batavia. What they expect to find in them is more than we can tell—perhaps chickens!

5. The Dutch traders were the original cause of this extraordinary vigilance. These people were accustomed to practise every art for the purpose of smuggling goods into their factory, and, in particular, made use of the ample folds of their garments to conceal small articles of value. These tricks sometimes led to amusing incidents.

6. On one occasion, the petty officer of a ship wished to smuggle a parrot, which animal is not among the licensed articles of trade, though it is not easy to understand how the religious or political system of Japan could be endangered by Poll's chattering. The man hid the parrot in that part of his dress which we call the *small clothes*, but which a Dutchman wears enormously large. There was room enough to hide, but unluckily, Poll began to talk in his lurking-place, and discovered the trick. After this, there was nothing which the Japanese would not suspect of a Dutchman under the temptation of smuggling.

7. The Chinese have, almost from time immemorial, traded to Japan, and are, perhaps, the only Asiatic people who have done this. Formerly, they ran with their vessels into Osacca harbor, although it is dangerous, on account of its rocks and sand-banks. The Portuguese showed them the way to Nangasaki, which, as we have said, is the only port into which they are admitted.

8. The Chinese and Japanese, although very near neighbors, as may be seen by looking upon the map, differ remarkably in their habits, language and religion. The Chinese wear frocks or wide jackets; the Japanese dress in gowns. The Chinese wear boots made of linen, and shoes with upper-leathers; the Japanese go bare-legged.

---

5. What was the cause of this vigilance ? 6. What anecdote is related of a parrot ? 7. What is said of the Chinese ? 8. How do they differ from the Japanese ?

CHAPTER LXVII.

GOVERNMENT, POPULATION AND PRODUCTIONS OF JAPAN.

1. The *Dairi* is the ecclesiastical chief, and may be called the pope of Japan. The veneration in which he is held, falls little short of the divine honors which are paid to the gods themselves. He seldom goes out of his palace, his person being considered too sacred to be exposed to the sun and air, and still less to the profane view of any human creature. If at any time he has any absolute necessity for going abroad, he is carried upon men's shoulders, that he may not touch the earth.

2. The Dairi is born, lives and dies within the precincts of his court. the limits of which he never passes during his whole life. His hair, nails and beard are accounted so sacred, that they are never suffered to be cut by daylight; this is always done at night, by stealth, when he is asleep. But the most ludicrous of all these absurd customs is this: he never eats twice off the same plate, nor uses any vessel for his meals a second time: they are all broken to pieces immediately after they have been used, to prevent their falling into unhallowed hands!

3. This regular *smashing* of cups and dishes after breakfast, dinner and supper, must, to our conception, be a highly amusing scene. But the Japanese use a precaution to save themselves a part of the cost of this very expensive as well as ridiculous custom:—they take care that his holiness shall be served on very cheap crockery.

4. It is scarcely to be believed what numbers of people are constantly travelling upon the roads in Japan; they are indeed often as much crowded as the streets of the most populous cities in Europe. One would suppose all Japan was out of doors and in motion, hurrying

---

Chapter LXVII.—*Questions.*—1. What veneration is paid to the Dairi? 2. What are the particulars of his life and habits? 3. What is said of his crockery? 4. What is said of travelling in Japan? To what is this owing?

to and fro. This is owing to the extraordinary population of the country, and the travelling propensities of the inhabitants, in which they seem to exceed all other people, even those of our country.

5. The princes and lords of the empire are required to visit the capital every year and pay their homage to the monarch. On these occasions they are always attended by an immense retinue, who fill up the roads in going and coming, and make an extraordinary display of pomp and magnificence. Some of these trains occupy several days in passing through a town.

6. It is a most striking spectacle to behold these vast bodies of men, sometimes 20,000 in number, mostly clad in black silk, marching in regular order, the whole preserving a decent and becoming gravity, and keeping so profound a silence, that not the least noise is to be heard, save from the trampling of the horses and men, and the rustling of so many silk gowns together.

7. The *Urusi*, or varnish-tree, is one of the noblest and most useful productions of this country. This tree not only grows wild in every part of Japan, but is cultivated in nurseries for its valuable qualities. It affords a milky juice which oozes out of the tree on its bark being cut. When first drawn it is of a lightish color, about the consistence of cream, but it grows thick and black on being exposed to the air.

8. This varnish is so transparent, that when laid pure and unmixed upon wooden furniture, every vein and knot in the wood may be seen through it. Generally, the article to be varnished is prepared by a ground of some dark color, which gives it a power of reflection like a mirror. Sometimes gold leaf ground fine is mixed with the varnish, which produces a very brilliant effect.

9. These lacquered articles are generally ornamented with gold and silver flowers. Of this beautiful work no adequate idea can be formed from the specimens commonly seen in Europe. What is really fine cannot be purchased by foreigners, and is not brought to this country.

---

5. What is said of the princes and lords? 6. What spectacle do they exhibit? 7. What is said of the varnish tree? 8. How is the varnish used? 9. What is said of lacquered articles?

10. Sometimes the Dutch at Nangasaki get some articles as presents from their Japanese friends; and these are mostly deposited in the Royal Museum at the Hague, in Holland. They would be esteemed scarcely second-rate articles in Japan, but are vastly superior to anything else of the kind in any other part of the world.

RUSSIA IN ASIA.

CHAPTER LXVIII.

SIBERIA—HISTORICAL SKETCH.

1. SIBERIA* occupies nearly a third part of Asia, having the Frozen Ocean on the north, Tartary and the Chinese territories on the south; and extending east

---

* Russia in Asia includes the Caucasian countries and Siberia. The former lie between the Black and Caspian Seas, on both sides of the Caucasian Mountains. The Circassians inhabit the northern side of these mountains. They are a vigorous race, famed for their love of independence and vigor in maintaining it. Many of the girls are sold to merchants, who take them to Turkey and Persia, where they are bought by rich men as slaves or wives for the harem. The Georgians occupy the southern slope of the mountains. The country is noted for its beauty and fertility. The people resemble the Circassians. Teflis is the capital.

Siberia is a cold region, to which the Russian emperor exiles those who offend him. This immense territory is a flat, cold, desolate region, occupied by several small tribes of people, nearly in a savage state. Among them are the Ostiaks, Samoiedes, Tungouses, Buraits, Koriaks, Yakoutes, Kamtscadales, &c. They live chiefly by hunting and fishing. They are short of stature, and resemble the Esquimaux. The Russians have several settlements here, and derive from the territory gold, silver, and copper, and a great variety of rich furs. Tobolsk is the capital, where most of the exiles live, though many of them are doomed to toilsome service in the mines, or in fur-hunting.

---

10. What of those obtained by the Dutch?
CHAPTER LXVIII.—*Questions.*—1. Describe Siberia.

and west from Europe to Bhering's Straits, which separate it from America. It is thinly inhabited, by small tribes of people, in a savage or barbarous state, though the Russians have settlements among them.

2. These rude and barren regions have hardly attracted the notice of the historian till very recent times. The ancients were ignorant that such a country existed, and imagined the greater part of this space to be covered by an unexplored ocean.

3. The Tartars, in the 13th century, made conquests in this country, and founded a sort of kingdom on the river Obi. This was called Siberia from its capital town, Sibir. For 300 years later, nothing was known in Europe of this country.

4. When Russia shook off the Tartar yoke and began to attain political power, some attempt was made to explore Siberia from the port of Archangel on the White Sea. The Samoiedes, inhabiting the district on the lower Obi and the shores of the Frozen Ocean, were accustomed to visit the banks of the Dwina, to exchange their skins and furs for Dutch toys and other articles.

5. An enterprising individual, named Strogonoff, conceived the project of extending this trade by penetrating into the regions from whence these furs were brought. He succeeded in the undertaking, and obtained considerable wealth by the traffic.

6. At lengh he persuaded some of the chief Samoiedes to accompany him to Moscow. The spectacle of the pomp and luxury of the Russian court is said to have so strongly affected the minds of these simple people, that they agreed to acknowledge the supremacy of the czar, and pay him a tribute of furs.

7. The Russians soon improved this new power by erecting forts on the Obi; and this district was made a place of banishment for criminals. In the latter part of the 16th century, Ivan Vassilevitch II., having expelled the Tartars from his dominions beyond the Cas-

---

2. What did the ancients know of this country? 3. What was done by the Tartars? 4. What by the Russians and Samoiedes? 5. What by Strogonoff? 6. What of the Samoiedes at Moscow? 7. What was done by the Russians on the Obi?

pian Sea, encountered the hostilities of a daring horde of barbarians named Cossacks. It required the exertion of all his military force to overthrow them.

8. A chieftain of this tribe, named Yermak, with a band of 6,000 followers, refused to submit, and fled eastward into Siberia. Attempting to establish themselves there, they found an enemy in the Tartar prince who held the dominion of that region.

9. The Cossacks, however, gained a complete victory over him, and Yermak took possession of Sibir, the Tartar capital, which secured him the possession of a more extensive kingdom than the one he had lost. Being still pursued, however, by the arms of the Russians, he was obliged to secure his possession by acknowledging the supremacy of the czar and reigning as his viceroy.

10. Yermak soon after lost his life in a war with the Tartars, and the dominion of Siberia fell entirely to the Russian prince. By successive expeditions, the Russians at length pushed their discoveries eastward to Bhering's Straits, and established their authority, with more or less completeness, over the multitude of rude tribes by which this vast expanse of territory is peopled.

11. Siberia is now principally known to the rest of the world as a place of banishment for criminals. In several of the towns and villages there is some refinement of manners; but the rustic population lead a sort of patriarchal life, and the hunters are little better than savages. The Cossacks form the military force by which the country is held in subjection.

---

8. What by Yermak? 9. What by the Cossacks? 10. What is said of the conquest of Siberia by the Russians? 11. What is the present state of Siberia?

CHAPTER LXIX.

SKETCHES AND ANECDOTES OF SIBERIA.

Natives of Siberia.

1. EVERY reader has heard of Siberia as a place of exile: and the name of this country suggests ideas of solitary deserts, excessive cold, dreariness, pain and misery. Siberia, in fact, presents to the view, extensive plains where the soil remains frozen many feet deep, innumerable rivers which are closed by a winter lasting eight months in the year: wide marshes exhaling, in summer, a pestilential air: barren mountains whose sides are concealed under a mantle of perpetual snow. The whole region may be regarded as a desert which is scarcely warmed by the summer sun, but continues

CHAPTER LXIX.—*Questions.*—1. What is the general idea which we have of Siberia? What scenes does it present?

throughout the year shrouded with a pale gray sky, or enveloped in driving storms of snow.

2. Siberia is the place of banishment for criminals and unfortunate persons in the Russian empire. It is an immense dungeon, where the most ferocious robbers and murderers are to be seen by the side of the unfortunate merchant, who on account of an error in his books is regarded as a bankrupt. The unhappy exiles are first sent to Moscow, where they are kept some days in prison. Each man is then shaved on one half of his head: a jacket of many colors is put on him, and his feet are secured by chains. They are then placed in carts which carry them over the snow, the swollen rivers, the broken roads and rugged hills, to the Siberian desert, where they are to submit to the punishment assigned them.

3. Criminals of the deepest dye are condemned to hard labor. These are employed in working the mines. At night they are shut up in houses surrounded by fortifications—a very useless precaution—for the irons which load their feet, and the soldiers stationed around them, are sufficient to prevent them from escaping. Bread, water and salt fish are all their nourishment. The whip and the cudgel are constantly employed to stimulate them to labor.

4. In the district of Tomsk, at the foot of the Altaian mountains, the interior of the silver mines presents a labyrinth of galleries supported by timbers or cut out of the solid rock. The water which flows down from the mountain, puts in motion enormous wheels which serve to raise up the ore. In the depths of these dark and damp caverns the criminals pass a great portion of their existence. It is almost impossible to work in the winter. In order to find the way to the mines, the people are obliged to set up poles in the deep snow to serve as guide-posts.

5. But mining is not the only laborious work to which the criminals are subjected. Some are employed in

---

2. To what use is it applied? How are the exiles carried off? 3. How are the worst criminals employed? 4. What is said of the silver mines of Tomsk? What of the labor of the miners? 5. What other occupation is assigned to the exiles?

hunting animals for their fur. They penetrate into the almost uninhabitable deserts of the north and east, which nature has rendered hardly accessible to man. They sometimes die of hunger when their stock of dry fish is expended, and when the severity of the weather prevents them from hunting or fishing.

6. Criminals of a lighter degree, and those exiled for political offences, are treated with less severity, but the hardships of these are sufficiently painful. No allowance is made for the mode of life to which an exile has been accustomed. Many of them die of fatigue on the way to Siberia.

7. Kotzebue, the German author, during his residence in Russia was arrested by the government without his knowing the cause. He was transported to Siberia, where he was treated in the most capricious manner; sometimes being exposed to great hardships and privations, and at other times being allowed the privilege of going about freely among the people of the different towns where he resided. As he was a man considerably distinguished in literature, he was often treated with much attention by the Russian officers.

8. He thus describes his occupation at Tobolsk: "Towards noon I usually walked out or climbed the rocks that surround the city, and which the torrents have worn into a variety of picturesque forms. From thence I surveyed the great sheet of water that deluged the environs, and the thick forest that skirted the horizon on every side. The governor with whom I dined almost every day, was far from being happy. Often when seated beside each other in his summer-house, we cast our eyes over the vast expanse of the waters and contemplated the immense forests beyond them.

9. "One day, giving free utterance to his feelings, he said to me, stretching forth his hand, 'Do you see those forests? They extend to the Frozen Ocean. The foot of man has not yet trodden them: they are inhabited solely by wild beasts. My government contains more territory than Germany, France and Turkey in Europe

---

6. What is said of other criminals? 7. What of Kotzebue? How was he treated? 8. How does he describe his occupations at Tobolsk? 9. What description did the governor give him of his government? What of his situation and feelings?

put together: yet, what advantage does it afford me? Scarcely a day passes without producing some new spectacle of misery with which I cannot, must not condole, while the distresses of the sufferers rend my heart. A heavy responsibility lies upon me. A mere accident which no human prudence could foresee or avert—a secret information, would be sufficient to deprive me of my employment, my honor and my liberty! And what indemnity have I for all this? A desert country, a severe climate and continual intercourse with suffering and unhappy fellow-creatures!"

10. An officer of the Russian police goes to a man against whom the government has any suspicion, and arrests him in the name of the Emperor. He is immediately carried off to Siberia, without being allowed to take leave of his family or to make any preparation for his journey, even so far as furnishing himself with clothing to protect him from the cold. Shame, misery and despair follow him into that country. Even the exile who is banished on mere suspicion carries with him a degree of reprobation. Every one avoids him, if not for his supposed crime, at least for the fear which the despotic government strikes into all Russians. These people are so distrustful, that when you ask them the most indifferent things about the government, they only reply "God knows it and the Emperor."

11. Among the most unfortunate exiles are the Poles who shared in the insurrection of 1830. The implacable resentment of the Emperor Nicholas banished them to Siberia with the worst criminals. For them there is neither clemency nor pity. Persecuted far and near, they find among the Russians who are exiled with them, enemies always ready to augment the cruelties of their official executioners. Despised by some, ill-treated by others, they have no other refuge than the resignation and the courage of martyrs. Happy are those who find an early death from hard labor, disease, or the rigor of the horrible climate.

---

10. What is said of arrests on suspicion? What is the situation of the exile in Siberia? 11. What is said of the Polish exiles? What peculiar sufferings do they endure?

CHAPTER LXX.

THE CAUCASIAN COUNTRIES—COLCHIS, IBERIA—THE GOLDEN FLEECE, ETC.

1. THESE countries take their name from the Caucasus, a group of mountain chains between the Black Sea and the Caspian. These mountains are very lofty, rugged, and for the most part covered with forests. The ancients called these countries *Colchis, Iberia* and *Albania*. At present they bear the names of Circassia, Georgia and Mingrelia.

2. The finest specimens of the human race are found among the Circassians, on which account the Europeans and some kindred Asiatic tribes are denominated the Caucasian race. This race of men have surpassed all others in the world for intellectual power, and the high degree to which they have carried all the arts of civilization.

3. The Caucasian countries were very imperfectly known to the ancients, and consequently their accounts of them were mixed with many extravagant fables. They believed that Prometheus, who stole fire from heaven, was chained to a lofty mountain, here, as a punishment for the theft. This country was also the scene of the celebrated story of the Golden Fleece, which is as follows:

4. In the kingdom of Colchis, on the shores of the Euxine or Black Sea, there existed a great treasure of some sort, which the Greeks called a *Golden Fleece*, and believed it to have been taken from a ram on which a person named Phryxus was transported from Greece to that distant country. This story of the golden fleece was circulated throughout the Grecian States, and caused an excitement among the young men of that country exactly like the "gold fever" which has pre-

---

CHAPTER LXX.—*Questions.*—1. Describe the Caucasian countries. What were their ancient names? What the modern? 2. What is said of the Circassians, and of the Caucasian race? 3. What did the ancients know and relate of these countries? 4. What was the Golden Fleece? What excitement did it cause in Greece?

vailed in the United States in respect to California.

5. All the ardent and adventurous youths were eager to set out for Colchis in search of the golden fleece, which was supposed to be rich enough to make the fortune of a whole army of adventurers. Accordingly a ship-builder named Argus, constructed a vessel of a very large size for that age, though she would be reckoned among the small craft of the present day. This vessel was named after him, the *Argo*. A company of fifty young men embarked in her, and were called from the name of the vessel, the *Argonauts*.

6. Jason the son of Eson, King of Iolcos, in Thessaly, took the command. Navigation was very little understood by the Greeks in those days, and none of these mariners had before this time ventured into the Black Sea, the entrance to which was believed to be guarded by certain terrific craggy rocks, called the *Symplegades*, which means "dashing together." These rocks were represented as floating on the water, and it was believed that when any ship or boat attempted to pass between them, they dashed together with such velocity and force, that not even a bird upon the wing could escape.

7. Such appalling stories made the enterprise of the Argonauts seem a most dangerous and desperate undertaking, and they approached the Symplegades with as much apprehension as our modern Californian adventurers come in sight of Cape Horn. When they first saw these terrible rocks they let fly a pigeon to make trial whether the bird could fly through, in which case they were resolved to attempt a passage.

8. The pigeon darted off and passed through the rocks, but lost its tail in the exploit. The Argonauts were encouraged by this success, and pulled at the oars with all their might. The rocks dashed together as they passed, and carried away the rudder of the Argo and part of her stern, but the vessel made good her

---

5. What enterprise was projected in consequence? What was the Argo? 6. Who commanded her? What is said of the Symplegades? 7. What experiment did the Argonauts try before passing through the rocks? 8. How did it succeed?

passage, on which it is said, the rocks immediately became fixed and have not moved to the present day! The strait is now called the Bosphorus.

9. The Argonauts steered eastward along the shore of the Euxine, and arrived at the river Phasis, in Colchis. Here they informed the inhabitants that they were come in search of the golden fleece. Ætes, the king of the country, hearing of this, sent to inform them that the golden fleece was hanging on a tree in the Sacred Grove of Mars, and that they might carry it away on this condition.

10. He had in his farm-yard two furious bulls with brazen hoofs, and whose nostrils breathed fiery flames. These animals they were to yoke together and plough an acre of ground with them, part of which they were to sow with the teeth of the dragon, slain by Cadmus, which had the power of producing a crop of armed men. Although this was an undertaking which surpassed anything ever, before or since, proposed, as worthy of a premium at a cattle-show—Jason, the leader of the Argonauts, undertook it.

11. It is said that Medea, the daughter of Ætes, fell in love with Jason, and assisted him to accomplish his task by her knowledge of sorcery. When the work was done, the king refused to give up the golden fleece; but by the help of Medea, Jason got possession of it, and escaped with her and the other Argonauts to Greece. Such is the renowned story of the golden fleece; but the Greeks, unfortunately, never told us what they did with their wonderful treasure, nor whether it turned out to be worth all the pains they took to go after it.

12. There have been many different explanations of the story. Some suppose the Argonauts went in search of a golden mine. Others think that the fine wool of Colchis constituted the great treasure, and that the Argonautic expedition was a trading voyage for that article; but this matter cannot now be determined.

---

9. Where did the Argonauts land? Where did they find the Golden Fleece? 10. What condition did Ætes propose? 11. How did Jason succeed in it? What was the result of the Argonautic expedition? 12. How is this story explained?

13. The Caucasian countries continued to be very little known to the rest of the world, even after the Romans had conquered Asia Minor. These rugged and inaccessible tracts served occasionally as the refuge of the vanquished, while they deterred even the boldest conquerors from attempting to subdue them. The Circassians have maintained their independence to the present day, notwithstanding the repeated efforts of the Russians to subjugate them.

Circassians.

14. The Georgians for a long time carried on a defensive war against the Persians. They then became tributary to the Czar of Russia, and about half a century ago, were incorporated into the Russian empire. Mingrelia still enjoys its own hereditary chiefs, but these princes acknowledge themselves the vassals of Russia.

---

13. What of the history of the Caucasian countries? What is said of the Circassians? 14. The Georgians—the Mingrelians?

HINDOSTAN.*

CHAPTER LXXI.

THE ANCIENT HINDOOS—THEIR TRADITIONS.

A Brahmin expounding the Veda.

1. The region known to the ancients by the name of *India*, and now most commonly by the Persian appel-

---

* Hindostan is celebrated for its rich products, its vast population, and its singular religion. The climate of this country is chiefly that of the torrid zone. Its products are cotton, silk, opium, tobacco, indigo, coffee, pepper, cinnamon, and other spices. Among the fruits are the mango, orange, grape, melons, &c. No part of the world offers a more luxuriant display of flowers than this. In the vales of Cashmere, the air is perfumed with roses. The country yields every variety of the palm, and besides the common fruits of Europe, there are many peculiar to the climate. In mineral wealth, India is one of the richest coun-

---

Chapter LXXI.—*Questions.*—1. What is said of ancient India?

lation of *Hindostan*, has always been the most celebrated country of the East. In every age it has been the seat of oriental pomp, of a peculiar civilization, and of a commerce supported by richer products than that of any other country, ancient or modern.

2. For a very long period of time Hindostan has been the theatre of absolute power exercised by foreign mili-

tries in the world. The animal kingdom is equally varied. Monkeys make their appearance everywhere in troops; serpents swarm in the forests and the gardens, and even visit the houses. The birds are innumerable; fifty kinds of parrots are known; and the flaunting peacock, here in its original country, appears in enormous flocks. The manufactures of silk and cotton, in Hindostan, have been long celebrated. The shawls of Cashmere are unrivalled. Gold is wrought, and precious stones set with great skill by the Hindoos. The diamonds of Golconda are the best in the world. Gold, iron, tin, and zinc, are among the mineral products of the country.

Religion and law combine to divide the people into four castes; 1st, Brahmins, or priests; 2d, Rajah-pootras, or soldiers; 3d, Vaisgas, or merchants and farmers; and 4th, Sudras, or laborers. These do not eat or drink together, nor intermarry; and if any one violates the rules of his caste, he becomes an outcast, or Pariah. The priests exercise the most unlimited sway over the people, who are in the highest degree ignorant and superstitious. The religion of the Hindoos teaches that Brahma is the supreme God, with millions of inferior deities. It also instructs the people to worship the various rivers, cows, apes, &c. In their temples are images, some of men, and some of brutes, before whom the people pay their adorations.

Christian missionaries, from Europe and America, have labored with great zeal and some success, in Hindostan. The Hindoos are a gentle, indolent, and contented people, living from age to age with unchanging devotion to the religion and customs of their fathers.

The greater part of Hindostan is now under the government of the British East India Company. The whole number of Europeans in Hindostan, who govern one hundred and thirty millions, do not probably exceed fifty thousand. Calcutta the capital, and principal residence of the British in India, is on a branch of the Ganges. Benares is the Holy City of the Hindoos. Delhi, the famous capital of the Mogul emperors, has a magnificent mosque. Cashmere is famed for its shawls, made of the hair of the Thibet goat. Bombay on an island, is the western capital of British India. Ceylon is a fine island at the southern extremity of Hindostan.

2. Of its ancient power?

THE ANCIENT HINDOOS. 163

tary potentates. It presents, however, many peculiarities distinguishing it from an ordinary despotism.

3. The basis of its population still consists of that remarkable native race, who, during a subjection of thousands of years have retained, unaltered, all the features of their original character. They are divided into four classes or *castes:* 1, the Brahmins or priests; 2, the soldiers; 3, the merchants and farmers; 4, the laborers.

4. These castes are forbidden to intermarry, or even to eat or drink together, and every person must belong to the same caste as his parents.

5. The Hindoos preserve in full force that earliest form of government—the village constitution; and their attachment to this appears to have been rendered stronger by the absence of every other political right and distinction.

6. When India became known to the Greeks by the conquests of Alexander, its inhabitants were found in very nearly the same state of civilization as the Hindoos of the present day. We may, therefore, fairly conclude that this civilized state must then have been many centuries in existence, otherwise it could not have been so complete and so permanent in its influence.

7. All the Hindoo traditions unite in representing the neighborhood of the Ganges as the cradle of their race. Their most ancient records intimate that the first kingdoms in this sacred spot were founded by persons who came from the north.

8. The first authentic knowledge of India, however, is afforded by the invasion of Alexander. The country was then the seat of an extensive empire, but it was divided among a number of small states. There seem to have been two great dynasties here in ancient times, the one claiming an origin from the sun, and the other from the moon: the former was established at Oude and the latter at Delhi.

---

3. Its population? 4. The castes? 5. The village constitution? 6. What is said of the Hindoos of Alexander's time? 7. What was the cradle of the Hindoo race? 8. What is said of the government in the time of Alexander?

CHAPTER LXXII.

BUDDHISM IN THE EAST—THE RAJAHS—CEYLON.

1. About half a century before Christ, a prince named Vicramaditya or Bickermagit, became the sovereign of all India. He ruled with such extraordinary splendor and success, that his reign forms an important era in oriental history. But towards the close of his life, he was conquered by Shahpoor, king of Persia, and Hindostan became united to the Persian empire.

2. The Hindoo accounts of Vicramaditya contain the most extravagant fables; and all that we can learn with certainty is, that this prince was a sedulous upholder of the influence of the Brahmins.

3. These, like the priests in Egypt, exercised an indirect sovereignty over the other classes of society. The kings were selected from the warrior caste, but the Brahmins restrained the power of the sovereign by religious enactments and institutions, which brought both public and private affairs under their cognisance.

4. At a very early but uncertain period, the religious institutions of the Brahmins were opposed by a reformer named Boodh, or Buddha, who rejected the Vedas or sacred Brahminical books, bloody sacrifices and the distinction of castes. His followers, called Buddhists, must have been both numerous and powerful in very remote ages, for a great number of the oldest rock temples in Hindostan are dedicated to him.

5. At some uncertain period, but probably not much later than the twelfth century, nor earlier than the fourth, A.D., the Buddhists were expelled from Hindostan by the Brahmins. They sought shelter in Ceylon, in the mountains of the north, in the countries beyond the Ganges, in Tartary and China, where their religion had been previously preached by active missionaries.

Chapter LXXII.—*Questions.*—1. What is said of Vicramaditya and Shahpoor? 2. Hindoo fables? 3. Brahmins? 4. Who was Boodh? 5. When were the Buddhists expelled from Hindostan?

THE RAJAHS—CEYLON.

6. By the persecutions exercised upon the Buddhists in their native country, a great part of the literature of India has been lost. During a period of above a thousand years, or from the reign of Vicramaditya to the invasion of the Mahometans, Hindostan appears to have been divided into a number of petty independent states.

7. In these, the Rajahs, or kings, were completely under the influence of the Brahmins. As the royal power declined, the rules of caste, on which the influence of the hereditary priesthood depended, were rendered more severe. The Brahmins arrogated to themselves the exclusive privilege of studying and expounding the Vedas.

8. As these books are the source of all Hindoo learning, whether religious or scientific, the priesthood thus obtained a monopoly of knowledge. Brahmins alone could exercise the medical art. They alone, also, had the right to interpret the laws, to offer sacrifices, and to give counsel to the sovereign.

9. The large and fertile island of Ceylon was not known to Europe before the time of Alexander. It was formerly called Taprobana. In the Arabian Nights it is called Sirendib. The Egyptians seem not to have visited the Coromandel coast on this island till the regular changing of the monsoons or trade-winds had been discovered.

10. In the reign of the Roman emperor Claudius, an ambassador was sent from Ceylon to Rome, and the island afterwards became a mart of trade for the commodities produced in the countries beyond the Ganges.

---

6. What followed the persecution of the Buddhists? 7. What is said of the Rajahs? 8. The Vedas? 9. Ceylon? 10. Its trade?

CHAPTER LXXIII.

MAHMOUD OF GHIZNI—AURUNGZEBE.

1. From the time of the Roman conquests in Asia, till the beginning of the 12th century, the commercial route of communication between Europe and Hindostan continued essentially the same. The ancient nations of the West were contented with trafficking in that quarter, without indulging in schemes of conquest or colonization.

2. Hindostan, however, was destined to suffer from the ravages of eastern conquerors. The invasion of Mahmoud, of Ghizni, whom we have already mentioned, forms the era at which authentic history commences in this country. The bold and hardy population which inhabit the mountains of Afghanistan enabled Mahmoud to carry his arms victoriously over many of the neighboring countries, and to erect a strong military empire in the region, anciently known under the name of Bactria.

3. This obtained the name of the Empire of Ghizni, from the capital Ghizni, or Gazna, which stood near the source of the Indus. By successive invasions of Hindostan during the early part of the 11th century, Mahmoud enriched himself with immense quantities of plunder, and he united all the western part of that country with nearly the whole of Persia and a great part of Tartary, to his empire.

4. The dynasty of Mahmoud in Hindostan was subverted by that of the Gaurs, a formidable race of mountaineers, who dwelt originally in the Hindoo Koosh, or Dark Mountains. Toward the end of the 12th century, they invaded Hindostan and founded an empire there.

5. Kuttub, an adventurer, who from a slave became emperor, transferred the seat of the empire from Lahore to Delhi. Mahometanism had been introduced with the

---

Chapter LXXIII.—*Questions.*—1. What is said of the commerce between Europe and Hindostan? 2. Of Mahmoud of Ghizni and the Afghans? 3. Of the empire of Ghizni? 4. What became of the dynasty of Mahmoud? 5. Who was Kuttub?

AURUNGZEBE.

Ghiznivide conquest. The Gaurs also established this religion at the court of their emperors.

6. At the close of the 14th century, Timour, or Tamerlane, the Tartar chieftain, invaded Hindostan with his Mongols; but it was more than a century afterwards that the Mongolian, or as it is more generally called, the *Mogul* empire, was founded here by the emperor Baber, one of Timour's descendants.

7. Under the two succeeding sovereigns, Akbar and Jehangire, this empire attained to a height of power and splendor scarcely equalled by any other monarchy, even of Asia. Under Aurungzebe, who succeeded these, and reigned through all the latter part of the 17th century, the Mogul empire extended from Chin India in the east, to Persia in the west; and from the Hindoo Koosh in the north, to the river Krishna in the south—comprising a population of eighty millions of souls.

8. This emperor's court displayed the most extraordinary wealth and magnificence. His hall of audience was roofed with silver, and wainscoted with gold. His throne was valued at five millions of dollars; the canopy and furniture of his state elephant at seventy-five millions, and the money in his treasury at one hundred and sixty millions.

9. But all this wealth had been obtained by plundering his own people or his neighbors; after his death, it was soon scattered abroad, and the power overthrown by which it had been accumulated.

10. Aurungzebe died in 1707. This event was followed by furious civil wars among his sons; and in 1739, the empire was invaded by Nadir Shah, of Persia. Delhi was sacked and burnt, and 100,000 of its inhabitants were put to the sword. The conqueror returned to Persia with an enormous plunder, comprising sixteen millions of dollars in money, seven millions in plate, the peacock throne, valued at five millions, the trappings of the state elephant, at fifty-five millions—in all three hundred and fifty millions of dollars! This sum was equal in value to more than one thousand millions, at this day and in this quarter of the world.

---

6. What is said of Timour? 7. Akbar, Jehangire, and Aurungzebe? 8. The emperor's court? 9. His wealth? 10. Who was Nadir Shah? What plunder did he obtain?

11. The conqueror left to the Mogul emperor all the territory east of the Indus; but, from this period, the empire remained the mere shadow of a mighty name. All the native tribes which, during the day of its power, had taken refuge in the mountains, now descended from their retreats to battle for the possession of the finest provinces of Hindostan. Among these tribes were the Mahrattas, who came from the Vindha Mountains, and the western Ghauts, overran the Deccan and penetrated to the imperial provinces of Delhi and Agra. In the south, Hyder Ali erected the powerful kingdom of Mysore.

12. The contending chiefs found it to be for their inteerst to allow the emperor, or the Great Mogul as he was called, to retain his throne and the shadow of authority. But while these rivals were fiercely contending for empire, a new power was rising, beneath which they were all destined to bow.

CHAPTER LXXIV.

THE PORTUGUESE IN INDIA.

1. When the Portuguese discovered the route to India by the Cape of Good Hope, their only object was commerce; but ere long they began to enlarge their schemes of traffic, and indulge in ambitious designs of territorial acquisition. Under the guidance of Albuquerque, a sagacious and enterprising commander, they procured a grant of land from one of the native princes, and built a strong fortress near Goa, on the western coast of Hindostan.

2. The Mahometans, who had hitherto engrossed the entire commerce of India, formed a league to expel the intruders, in which they were encouraged by the Venetians, who bought Indian spices and other goods from

---

11. What followed the invasion? 12. What is said of the Great Mogul?
Chapter LXXIV.—*Questions.*—1. How did the Portuguese establish themselves in India? 2. What was done by the Mahometans?

Arrival of the first Portuguese Fleet at Calicut.

the Arabs, with which they supplied the principal markets of Europe. This enterprise was defeated, and soon after, Albuquerque laid the foundation of the future supremacy of the Portuguese by reducing Goa, which subsequently became the seat of government.

3. He also subdued the city of Malacca and the island of Ormuz in the Persian Gulf. This last was the most remarkable of all the Portuguese settlements in the East. The island of Ormuz was originally nothing but a salt and barren rock at the entrance of the gulf, having no water except when the rain, which seldom falls, is collected in pools or cisterns; but its commodious situation for trade rendered it the most flourishing commercial mart in the eastern seas.

4. The harbor of Ormuz was frequented by shipping from all parts of the Indies, from the coasts of Africa and Arabia, while it enjoyed an extensive caravan trade with the interior Asiatic countries, through the opposite ports of Persia. The wealth, the splendor, and the

---

3. What is said of Malacca and Ormuz? Of the commerce and wealth of Ormuz?

concourse of traders at Ormuz during its flourishing condition, gave the world a memorable example of the wonderful power of commerce.

5. In the trading season, which lasted from January to March, and from August to November, there was not only an unparalleled activity of traffic at Ormuz, but a display of luxury and magnificence which seemed to realize the extravagances of fiction. The salt dust of the streets was concealed and kept down by neat mats and rich carpets; canvas awnings were extended from the roofs of the houses to exclude the scorching rays of the sun.

6. The rooms on the streets were opened, like shops, and adorned with Indian cabinets and piles of porcelain intermixed with odoriferous shrubs and flowers, set in gilt vases. Camels laden with skins of water stood at the corners of the streets, while the richest wines of Persia, the most costly perfumes and the choicest delicacies of Asia were poured forth in lavish profusion.

7. But this busy scene of wealth and prosperity was soon to pass away. The Portuguese became involved in hostilities with Shah Abbas, the most powerful of the Persian monarchs; they also met with formidable rivals in the English, who were now seeking to establish themselves in the East. The Persians and English made a combined attack upon Ormuz, and captured it in 1682.

8. All the wealth of the place, amounting to several millions in value, fell into the hands of the captors. Ormuz never recovered from this catastrophe: the trade of the port was transferred to other quarters, the city fell into decay, and the materials of its splendid edifices were taken away by Dutch vessels, as ballast. The island soon relapsed into its original condition of a barren and desolate rock. It now belongs to the Imaum of Muscat, who, on first taking possession of it, found about twenty houses on the island. Under his dominion, the place is said to be reviving.

---

5. Of the streets of the city? 6. Of the houses, &c.? 7. What caused the fall of Ormuz? 8. What was its ultimate fate? Its present condition?

CHAPTER LXXV.

THE FRENCH IN INDIA.

1. THE French were slower than their neighbors in prosecuting maritime enterprises. Francis I. and Henry III. issued edicts, exhorting their subjects to undertake long voyages; but either a want of enterprise in the people, or the inability of the government to afford pecuniary assistance, prevented any considerable efforts for mercantile enterprise or discovery.

2. At length, a French East India Company was formed, in 1616. But its first attempts at business were so discouraging, that the members resolved to abandon the trade with India, and direct their attention to the establishment of a settlement in the island of Madagascar. Here, however, they met with no permanent success.

3. Towards the close of the 17th century, they purchased the town of Pondicherry, in Hindostan, from the sovereign of Visapour, and began to form a settlement there with every encouraging prospect. Some trouble arose from the Dutch, who wrested this place from them in 1693, but it was restored at the peace of Ryswick, in 1697.

4. From this time, the prosperity of the colony continued to increase. The French captured from the Dutch the two African islands of Mauritius and Mascarenhas, since called the Isles of France and Bourbon; and this acquisition led them to hope that they might acquire an important share in eastern commerce.

5. A new career of ambition was opened to them by the sanguinary struggle which arose between the states formed out of the fragments of the Mogul empire. Dupleix, the French governor of Pondicherry, hoped, by embroiling the natives with each other, to obtain territorial acquisitions as the price of his assistance

---

CHAPTER LXXV.—*Questions.*—1. What French sovereigns first encouraged commerce? 2. What is said of the French East India Company? 3. Of Pondicherry? 4. Mauritius and Mascarenhas? 5. What was done by Dupleix?

to some of the combatants. The English adopted the same course of policy, and soon the ancient hostility between the two nations extended its influence to India.

6. The English were the conquerors in the struggle which ensued, and which ended in the almost total expulsion of the French from Hindostan, with the cession of most of their settlements to the English, at the peace of 1763. They afterwards intrigued with the native princes, Hyder Ali and Tippoo Sultan, against their successful rivals, but they have been utterly unable to regain any portion of their former influence.

CHAPTER LXXVI.

BRITISH INDIA.

British Governor-general of India.

1. THE English were behind most of the other European nations in making settlements in India; but their

---

6. What became of the French possessions in India?
CHAPTER LXXVI.—*Questions.*—1. When did the English begin their settlements in India?

success has been by far the most brilliant, and their eastern empire the most permanent. About the middle of the 17th century, they obtained a grant of land on the Coromandel coast, near Madras, where they built Fort St. George.

2. A few years later, they acquired from the Portuguese, by treaty, the island of Bombay, on the western coast of Hindostan. Near the close of the century, they formed a settlement at Calcutta, where the Mogul emperor granted important privileges of trade.

3. It was at this place that the dreadful catastrophe of the Black Hole occurred. The subah or viceroy of Bengal, being jealous of the English, attacked Calcutta in 1756. He captured the town and made prisoners of the English garrison. These men, 146 in number, were cast into a narrow dungeon, where they were crowded together during an intensely hot night. All of them, except 23, perished from heat and suffocation, after having suffered the most horrible agonies.

4. The foundation of the British empire in India was laid by Robert Clive, who went to that country as a private adventurer, about the middle of the eighteenth century, and soon acquired the supremacy in the government by his courage and talents. Through his intrigues, usurpations and treacheries, he was enabled to gain great possessions for the East India Company, in whose service he acted. He returned to England with immense wealth, and was made Lord Clive for his achievements.

5. Warren Hastings was governor-general of British India during the latter part of the 18th century. He also added much to the British power in that quarter. The unfortunate Hindoos were plundered and massacred without scruple in the course of these proceedings. Hastings was put on trial for high crimes and misdemeanors after his return to England, but was acquitted.

6. Hyder Ali, an intrepid and enterprising chieftain, made war against the British in the south of Hindostan,

---

2. When did they acquire Bombay and Calcutta? 3. What is said of the Black Hole? 4. Who laid the foundation of the British Empire in India? 5. What is said of Warren Hastings? 6. Of Hyder Ali and Tippoo Saib?

and nearly annihilated their power in that quarter. His son Tippoo inherited his hostile spirit against the foreigners, but did not possess the skill and experience of his father. After two obstinate wars, his career was terminated in 1799. His capital, Seringapatam, was taken, and Tippoo was killed.

7. The kingdom of Tippoo was seized by the English and divided between them and their allies. From that time to the present, the British have been engaged in wars with various nations of Hindostan and its frontiers, with the Mahrattas, the Pindarees, the Burmese, the Nepaulese, the Sikhs, the Belooches, the Afghans, &c.

8. In almost all these conflicts they have been successful and gained large tracts of territory, so that at the present day their supremacy in Hindostan is fully established.

9. The subjection of the Hindoos to the English is complete and almost universally peaceable. It may appear incredible that a hundred and thirty millions of men should submit to the domination of 30,000—for there are probably not more than this number of British in the country. But the character of the Hindoo is such that he is easily trained into an instrument for holding his own country in subjection.

10. The Asiatic soldier fights only for pay and plunder. He is attached only to the master whose bread he eats, and him he will defend against friends, country and family. Accordingly, the Sepoys or Hindoo troops commanded by British officers, are found by the latter nearly as trustworthy as Englishmen.

---

7. What is said of the British wars in India? 8. Of the British acquisitions? 9. Of the subjugation of the Hindoos? 10. What is the character of the Asiatic soldier?

FARTHER INDIA.

CHAPTER LXXVII.

DESCRIPTION OF CHIN INDIA—BURMAH.

BURMESE.

1. This region is called Farther India,* or India beyond the Ganges. It is an extensive maritime territory,

---

* Farther India, comprises several barbarous states and empires. Among these are Burmah, or the Burman empire, Siam, Anam, and several territories now under British sway. The people of these regions are chiefly of dark or yellow complexions, and bear a resemblance alike to the Hindoos and Chinese. The governments are despotisms; the religion, various forms of superstition. The mass of the people are ignorant and degraded.

Burmah is the leading kingdom; the people evincing more activity and vigor than the other natives. The emperor keeps a white elephant superbly dressed, which is an object of reverence to the people. Ava, on the Irawaddy, is the capital. Rangoon

---

Chapter LXXVII.—*Questions.*—1. Describe Farther India.

throwing out long peninsular tracts into the Indian Ocean. It is separated from Hindostan on the west by the Bay of Bengal, and has China and Thibet on the north. It comprises Cochin-China, the Burman empire, Tonquin, Pegu, Cambodia, Laos, Siam, and the peninsula of Malacca.

2. The most important division is the Burman empire, which now includes the ancient kingdoms of Ava, Pegu and Arracan. The knowledge of the ancients respecting this part of the world amounted to little. The Golden Chersonese, mentioned by Ptolemy, is supposed to be Malacca, but no description in the ancient geographies shows any accurate acquaintance with Farther India.

3. It was not till the 13th or 14th century that the moderns obtained any distinct notions of these fertile and populous kingdoms, some of which are said to have been founded centuries before the Christian era. The Buddhist religion is supposed to have been introduced into these countries B. C. 440, but the early annals of the natives are filled with wild and extravagant fables.

4. Ava, or the Burman empire, appears to have undergone more vicissitudes than any other of the Chin Indian kingdoms. It comprises three states that were originally separate and independent, namely; Ava, or Burmah, Arracan and Pegu. For a considerable period, a struggle for the supremacy was carried on among these powers, each in its turn gaining the ascendency.

---

is celebrated for its temples. The king of Cochin-China has conquered Cambodia, and other territories, thus founding the empire of Anam, of which Hue is the capital. Siam is a populous kingdom of some stability, the people devoting their attention to agriculture and commerce. Bankok is the chief city.

Malacca, the original country of the Malays, with the territories of Assam and Arracan, has been recently wrested from the Burmese empire by the British East India Company. Malacca is a long peninsula, a large portion of which is covered with forests. These are infested with clouds of mosquitoes; serpents abound; and leopards, tigers, and crocodiles render the path of the traveller a scene of constant danger.

Its divisions. 2. What is said of the Burman empire? What did the ancients know of it? 3. What is said of its early history? What religion was established here? 4. What is said of Ava?

5. When these countries first became known to Europeans by the arrival of the Portuguese in India, Pegu was the ruling state, and its court displayed considerable pomp. About the middle of the 16th century, the Burmans rebelled against this authority, and not only established their own independence, but subdued their former masters.

6. This supremacy continued till about the middle of the 18th century, when the Peguans, having obtained arms and military leaders from the Dutch and Portuguese, turned them against the Burmans, gained many victories, and finally reduced the capital, making prisoner of Dweepdee, the last of a long line of Burman kings.

7. The Burmese, however, although conquered by the Peguan armies, were by no means completely crushed, and a reaction soon arose among this brave and energetic people. Alompra, a man of humble birth, collected a band of his countrymen, and carried on, for some time, a desultory warfare against the invaders.

8. His forces gradually increased, and he was at length able, by a sudden and unexpected attack, to make himself master of the capital. A general insurrection was now raised against the king of Pegu. A powerful army sent by that prince to crush the revolt was totally defeated, and Alompra, following up his success, invaded Pegu and gained a series of victories, which put him in possession of the capital of that kingdom.

9. The Peguan dynasty was thus extinguished. The successor of Alompra was Shenbuyen. He suppressed a revolt of the Peguans, defeated the Chinese in a great battle, and gained possession of Siam, but was unable to retain any part of that monarchy except the provinces of Mergui and Tenasserim on the western coast of Malacca.

10. His brother, Namdogyee Pra, who afterwards ascended the throne, succeeded in annexing Arracan to the empire. The Burman dominion thus became extremely powerful, as its influence was also established

---

5. What of Pegu? 6. What success had the Peguans? 7. Who was Alompra? 8. What was his success? 9. What is said of the successors of Alompra? 10. How was the Burman empire extended?

over the territories of Cachar, Cassay, and others bordering on Bengal, through which it came in contact with the British territory.

11. Two proud and powerful states were not likely to be long in proximity without some collision. A series of misunderstandings at length produced an open rupture, and the British invaded the Burman territory with a large force in 1826. They captured Rangoon and Prome, and defeated a large Burmese army. The emperor seeing no chance of defending his capital, at length consented to a treaty, by which he ceded to the British Arracan, Mergui, Tavoy, and Tenasserim, besides paying them a large sum for the expenses of the war.

CHAPTER LXXVIII.

COCHIN-CHINA—SIAM.

COCHIN-CHINESE.

1. OF these countries little more than the name was known to Europe till the latter part of the last century,

---

11. What happened in the war with the British?
CHAPTER LXXVIII.—*Questions.*—1. When did Cochin-China and Siam become known to Europe?

when they were brought into notice by means of an important revolution. In 1774, Caung Shung the young king of Cochin-China, was dethroned and driven from his capital by three usurpers who assumed the supreme authority. The prince took refuge in a desert island, where he lived several years in extreme distress.

2. In the mean time, Adran, a French missionary in Cochin-China, who had aided him in accomplishing his escape, continued to support his cause, and spared no efforts to replace the young monarch on his throne. He made a voyage to France, to solicit the aid of the government for this purpose; but the disturbed state of the kingdom, in consequence of the revolution, obstructed this design.

3. Adran was, however, enabled to procure some aid in arms and officers for Caung Shung; and in 1790, this prince landed on the continent, was welcomed by his subjects, and restored to his authority. The circumstances under which his restoration had been accomplished, led him to form a strong attachment to Europeans, and to feel a desire to introduce those improvements, especially in the military art, by which they were so much distinguished above his own subjects.

4. Caung Shung organized a standing army and disciplined it in the European manner, and built a fleet of 300 gun-boats and a frigate, thus becoming master of a force unrivalled in this part of Asia. With this armament, he first conquered Tonquin, a kingdom greater and more populous than his own, and next Cambodia. In this manner he became sovereign of all that great range of territory which lies between the gulfs of Siam and Tonquin, and now constitutes a part of the empire of Cochin-China.

5. SIAM, consisting of a single great valley at the head of a wide gulf, and enclosed by two ranges of mountains, has maintained a more stable political character than any other of this cluster of kingdoms. It

---

Who was Caung Shung? 2. Who was Adran? 3. What success had Caung Shung? What was the consequence of his restoration? 4. What is said of his military power and conquests? 5. What is said of Siam?

was, indeed, subdued by the Burmese, in the height of their power; but on this occasion, as at other times, the strong national feeling of the Siamese impelled them to rise on the invaders and expel them from the country.

6. The Siamese have made considerable progress in the cultivation of the soil, and their country is famous for its excellent fruit. The neighborhood of Bankok, the capital, is like one great orchard. The Siamese elephants are the finest in the world.

CHAPTER LXXIX.

CAMBODIA—TONQUIN—LAOS.

1. CAMBODIA is very little known to us. The chief production of the country is the yellow pigment, *gamboge*. This is a resin obtained from the leaves and branches of a tree. The country is but indifferently peopled, and seems to be much declined from its former flourishing state.

2. The capital consists of but a single street, with one large temple. In its neighborhood are to be seen the ruins of an ancient city, the architecture of which exhibits something of the European style, while the ridges in the adjoining fields indicate that they have been under tillage.

3. There is said to be a large lake or inland sea in the interior. A great part of the country is inundated at certain seasons, and there are also extensive deserts. The sea-coast is generally low, sandy, covered with underwood, and washed by a very shallow sea.

4. A little tin and gold are exported; and the fields produce rice and other vegetable food. Many Japanese, Chinese and Malays are settled in this country. These last are scarcely distinguishable from the native Cambodians, who have dark yellow complexions and long black hair.

---

6. What of the people?
CHAPTER LXXIX.—*Questions.*—1. Describe Cambodia. 2. The capital. 3. What is the general appearance of the country? 4. What is said of the productions and inhabitants?

TONQUIN—LAOS.

5. TONQUIN borders upon China, from which empire it was separated in 1368. Its government has preserved those patriarchal forms of despotism which distinguish the great nations of Asia. Rank, honors and wealth are concentrated in the mandarins, literary and military. Here, as in China, the monarch annually celebrates a festival in honor of agriculture.

6. This nation, though less refined than the Chinese, seems to possess a greater degree of moral vigor: they have exhibited an impetuous bravery, and their history records some splendid instances of heroism and generosity. Their army, which exceeds 100,000 men, often defeats the Chinese. Their navy consists of 200 galleys, and is remarkable for the employment of a sort of Greek fire which burns under water.

7. The Gulf of Tonquin and the adjacent seas are noted for dreadful whirlwinds, called *tuffoons* or *typhoons*. After calm weather, they are announced by a small black cloud in the north-east, with a copper-colored margin, which gradually brightens till it becomes white and brilliant. This alarming appearance often precedes the hurricane, twelve hours. These dreadful winds seem to arise from the mutual opposition of the north wind coming down from the mountains, and the south wind proceeding from the ocean.

8. Nothing can exceed the fury of the tuffoons. They are accompanied with dreadful thunder, lightning and heavy rain. After five or six hours, a calm succeeds; but the hurricane soon returns in an opposite direction, with additional fury and continues for an equal space of time.

9. The kingdom of LAOS is separated from all the adjoining states by high mountains and thick forests. It has never been explored by a European, and offers a most interesting field for the researches of the first traveller who possesses sufficient courage and address to penetrate into it through the Burman dominions. It affords gold, musk, benzoin, rubies, topazes, pearls and other precious commodities.

---

5. What is said of Tonquin? 6. What is the character of the people? 7, 8. What is said of tuffoons? 9. What of Laos?

TRAVELS IN ASIA:

ILLUSTRATIVE OF

HISTORY, MANNERS, CUSTOMS, &c.

CHAPTER LXXX.

ADVENTURES OF THE FRENCH JESUITS IN CHINA.

1. In 1684, Louis XIV. of France sent an embassy of Jesuit friars to China, by the way of Siam. They spent a year at the court of this latter kingdom, and then embarked for Macao. On the voyage the vessel sprung a leak, and compelled them to land on the coast of Cambodia, where they set out to travel by land to Canton. They soon lost their way, and were entangled in trackless woods, where they found not a particle of food, nor any living thing except tigers, serpents, and

---

CHAPTER LXXX.—*Questions.*—1. When were the French Jesuits sent to China? What were their first adventures?

mosquitoes. After wandering for a fortnight and being reduced to the most miserable condition, they fortunately came to a small village, the inhabitants of which charitably reconducted them back to their vessel.

2. They returned to Siam, and in 1687 re-embarked in a Chinese junk for Ningpo. They suffered much from the superstitious habits of the Chinese sailors; no savory food was allowed to be eaten till it had first been offered to a little black idol; and the friars, who had scruples about tasting meat offered to idols, were obliged to live upon plain rice. They saw the sailors worshipping the very compass by which they steered, and even offering meat to it.

3. When the sea was rough, they threw into it little paper boats, hoping thus to amuse the waves and prevent them from attacking the vessel. When the storm grew violent, they burned feathers, hoping *by the smell* to drive away the demon that raised the wind. Through troubles like these they made their way to China.

4. After meeting with all sorts of impediments and mortifications in that country, they reached Pekin, where they were loaded with chains. They obtained favor at the court by a singular accident. One of the most important parts of Chinese state policy consists in the composition of the imperial calendar, prepared by the Tribunal of Astronomy, and exhibiting for every day the places of all the planets and that of the sun in the zodiac. It is presented with great pomp to all the members of the royal family and the officers of state, who receive it on their knees.

5. This work, indeed, is of indispensable use to every Chinese, as it affords the materials from which he calculates the lucky hour and minute for sowing, planting, shearing his sheep, cutting his hair, and almost every action of life.

6. The Chinese and Arabian astronomers having waited upon the emperor Kang-hi, with the calendar

---

2. How did they fare in a Chinese junk? 3. Describe the superstitions of the Chinese sailors. 4. What happened to the Jesuits in China? How did they obtain favor at the court? Describe the Chinese calendar. 5. Its use. 6. What discovery was made by the emperor?

which they had prepared, that prince had the sagacity to see that there was something wrong in it, without being able to discover what the error was. After some perplexity he bethought himself of the European priests, and ordered that their chains should be taken off, and that they should be conducted to the palace.

7. On examining the calendar, they found it erroneous, containing thirteen months in the year. The emperor immediately called a meeting of the Mandarins and the members of the high tribunals to deliberate on the subject. An assemblage took place, such as had never before been held upon an astronomical question, and one would have supposed that the very existence of the empire had been at stake.

8. The Jesuits explained the strange blunder that had been committed in the calendar, and the assembly being fully convinced of it, entreated them to contrive some means to cover it up and prevent the public from discovering it. They replied that they could not alter the heavens, and the emperor was obliged to issue his proclamation commanding all his loyal subjects not to have anything to do with a particular month which he named. The whole empire was thrown into great perplexity by this proceeding, and the people could not imagine what had become of so large a portion of time which seemed thus to be snatched out of their hands.

9. The Jesuits, for their superior knowledge, were placed at the head of the tribunal of astronomy, and had the sole direction of the calendar. The emperor, who was eager to acquire every kind of knowledge, and was not satisfied with that which China afforded, sought instruction in the European sciences of geometry, algebra, natural philosophy, astronomy, medicine, and anatomy. The Jesuits spent several years in composing lectures upon these subjects in the Mantchoo Tartar language, which they delivered twice a day at the palace.

10. They made great exertions to convey to Europe

---

7. What was the error in the calendar? How did the emperor behave on discovering it? 8. What was done at the assembly of the Mandarins? What proclamation was issued by the emperor? 9. How did the Jesuits succeed in China? 10. What information did they collect?

information concerning this vast empire. A body of them were employed to survey the different provinces, and to fix the leading positions by astronomical observations, so that our maps of China are constructed more accurately than those of almost any other country out of Europe.

11. As we have already remarked in the history of China, the Jesuits made many converts to Christianity in the empire, which roused the jealousy of the powerful men at court, and in the end caused the emperor to expel them from his dominions, with the exception of a small number who were retained at Pekin for their usefulness in regulating the calendar.

12. The Chinese converts to Christianity were cruelly persecuted, but the Christian religion was never entirely rooted out, and at the present day redoubled efforts are made by American and other missionaries to diffuse the Bible in this country and introduce the doctrines of the Christian religion.

CHAPTER LXXXI.

LORD MACARTNEY'S EMBASSY TO CHINA.

1. An embassy under Lord Macartney was sent by the British government to China in 1792. It was conveyed in a ship of war to the Yellow Sea, in order to avoid the delay and obstacles of a land journey from Canton. In navigating along the eastern coast, they came to the great archipelago of Chusan, consisting of upwards of 400 islands. Immense numbers of boats here surrounded the English ship, which was a strange object to the eyes of the Chinese. The English were equally astonished at the sight of the Chinese vessels.

2. The larger ones were of the most clumsy construction, being shaped like the new moon, with the

---

11. How were jealousies excited against them? 12. What has been the fortune of Christianity in China?

CHAPTER LXXXI.—*Questions.*—1. When did Lord Macartney go to China? What is said of the archipelago of Chusan? 2. The ships of the Chinese? The *tuffoons?*

head and stern rising to an enormous height. The masts bore each a single sail made of bamboo fibres, furling and unfurling like a fan. These awkward vessels thus awkwardly rigged, are accustomed to navigate the seas exposed to the *tuffoon,* a hurricane so furious that as the mariners in those seas affirm, " if ten thousand drums and as many trumpets were sounding at the same moment they would not be heard." It is said that ten or twelve thousand persons perish every year in this navigation.

3. When the English reached the mouth of the river Pei-ho, they found provisions and fruits sent down to them in great quantities by the care of the government, and thirty or forty vessels were lying ready to convey them up the stream. Their flags bore this inscription: " *The English ambassador carrying tribute to the emperor of China.*"

4. As they proceeded up the river the banks were crowded with spectators; the females had large branches of artificial flowers stuck in their hair; their faces were daubed with white paint; their eyelids were blackened, and their chins painted with vermilion spots. The abundant population of the country astonished the travellers. Not only the land but the water was thickly inhabited. In the course of ninety miles on the river they counted a thousand vessels fitted up as houses, each containing ten or twelve apartments sufficient to hold a family.

5. At length they landed and proceeded by land to Pekin. This city at first looked flat and uninteresting, being without the spires and domes which commonly decorate great capitals. On entering, however, the steets were found straight and broad, and the houses though only one story high, were painted with various colors and adorned with flags, so that the whole city had the appearance of a large encampment.

6. The crowd of movable workshops, the tents and booths for selling provisions, the processions of men in office, the funerals, the wedding-parties, fiddlers, jugglers,

---

3. What did the English see at the mouth of the Pei-ho? 4. In going up the river? What is said of the women? Of the population? 5. How did Pekin appear? 6. The crowd in that city?

conjurors, mountebanks, musicians, &c., composed so numerous and confused a crowd, that the guards of the embassy could scarcely make way through them with their whips.

7. The emperor was at Jehol in Tartary, where he had a hunting palace, and the embassy set out for that place. On their journey they were accommodated in palaces which had been built at regular stages for the accommodation of the emperor in his summer excursions into Tartary. On the fourth day they saw what appeared to be a line stretching over the whole extent of the mountainous horizon in the north. It was the Great Wall.

8. On approaching it, their astonishment was increased at seeing this immense structure carried over so rugged a barrier, ascending the highest mountains, and descending into the deepest valleys, with towers at the distance of every hundred steps. At Jehol Lord Macartney had an interview with the emperor, and presented him with the king of England's letter.

9. After this the emperor invited him to view the imperial gardens. The English were conducted through woods and lawns of the most magnificent character, extending for three miles, till they came to a lake so formed that the end of it appeared to be lost in the distance. Entering a splendid barge they sailed along this fine piece of water, which presented at every turn varied features of shore, bay, rock and forest. The artful arrangement of this was so carefully concealed that it appeared the grandest specimen of ornamented nature which the English had ever seen.

10. They landed at numerous pavilions filled with vases, porcelain, globes, orreries, clocks, &c., of such exquisite workmanship, and in such profusion, that the presents which the English had brought for the emperor, and which they thought would astonish the Chinese, seemed as nothing.

11. The embassy then began its journey homeward, bearing a letter from the emperor to the king of Eng-

---

7. What is said of the journey to Jehol? 8. Of the Great Wall? 9. Of the imperial gardens? The scenery here? 10. What did they find here? 11. What was the spectacle on the Hoang-ho?

land. They were struck with the grand spectacle exhibited by the Hoang-ho, or Yellow River—a very wide stream bordered with quays of marble and granite with continued ranges of houses, while both the river itself and the various canals branching out from it were covered with crowds of shipping.

12. The superstitious Chinese deemed it necessary to propitiate the genius of the Yellow River before they launched into its rapid waters. They accordingly made offerings of fowls, pigs, wine, oil, tea, flour, rice and salt, which were poured into the river, after which they thought it safe to embark. The river was yellow in color as well as by name, being as thick and muddy as if torrents of rain had just fallen, although it was a time of great drought.

13. A voyage of about a hundred miles brought them to the river Yang-tse-kiang, a grand and beautiful stream which flowed so gently that the Chinese thought no offering was requisite to keep it in good-humor. The appearance of the country was now superior to all they had previously seen. The fleets of vessels of every sort moving to and fro, the continued succession of towns and villages, the varied aspect and high cultivation of the lands, formed a most striking and agreeable picture.

14. On approaching Sou-tcheou-fou, they found the place so enormous in size that they sailed for three hours through the suburbs before they fairly reached the city. The inhabitants were dressed in silk, and everything indicated great wealth. They visited also the city of Hang-tchoo-foo, which the old traveller Marco Polo describes in its ancient glory under the name of Quensai. It was now seen in its decline, but even in this state it struck the English with admiration. They describe, in their narratives, the magic beauties of its lake, the numerous pleasure-parties which covered it, the gilded barges with floating streamers sailing to and fro, with the magnificent pavilions that studded its margin.

15. From this place they proceeded by land and water to Canton, where the embassy embarked and return-

---

12. What superstition was practised by the Chinese here?
13. What is said of the Yang-tse-kiang? 14. Of Sou-tcheou-fou?
15. Of the return of the embassy to Canton?

ed to England. This expedition cost the British government 400,000 dollars, while their expenses paid by the emperor for their travels and sojourn in China were estimated at 860,000 dollars. Notwithstanding this enormous cost the British gained no advantage from it, beyond the information respecting the country which is contained in the narratives of the expedition.

16. A second embassy in 1816 reesulted no better. Lord Amherst went to Pekin, where the officers of the government refused to admit him to the presence of the emperor unless he would perform the ceremony of the *Ko-tou*, or nine prostrations before the throne. This was too much for British pride, and the ambassador returned to Canton as wise as he went.

17. The ambassador found a triumphal arch which had been raised to celebrate his arrival, thrown down for the purpose of insulting him. A beggar who stood up, out of respect, as the British ambassador passed by, was ordered by the Chinese officers to sit down. At Canton an edict was published by the imperial authorities, bitterly reproaching the English for the disrespect they had shown in not performing the ceremonies demanded of them at Pekin. Such was the close of the last British embassy to the emperor of China.

CHAPTER LXXXII.

HARDWICKE'S TRAVELS TO THE SOURCE OF THE GANGES.

1. No object in the structure of the earth has more strongly excited the curiosity of mankind than the great rivers by which it is watered. Besides the rank which they hold among the grand features of the globe, their very aspect powerfully impresses the imagination. The mighty tide of the Ganges or the Nile, rolling on unal-

---

What was the cost of it? What benefit did it produce? 16. What happened to Lord Amherst's embassy? 17. In what manner was it treated by the Chinese?

CHAPTER LXXXII.—*Questions.*—1. What is remarked of great rivers?

tered, from age to age, amid all the revolutions of time and empire, must excite powerful emotions in the beholder.

Hindoos.

2. Of all the great rivers in Asia, none equals the fame of the Ganges. The magnificent plain which it waters, the lofty mountain-barrier from which it descends, and the mysterious obscurity which hangs about its origin, have given it a great name both in ancient and modern times. The British government in 1796 dispatched Captain Hardwicke to penetrate into the lofty regions of Northern India, for the purpose of discovering the source of this river. He was the first European who visited these regions.

---

2. What of the Ganges? When did Captain Hardwicke travel to discover the sources of this river?

3. At a town called Haridwar, on the upper Ganges, he found an immense number of Hindoo pilgrims assembled for the purpose of bathing in the river at a spot where the stream separates into three branches, and which is esteemed peculiarly sacred on that account. The crowd was estimated at two millions. From this quarter he ascended a range of lofty mountains skirted by vast forests.

4. Among the mountains were great torrents called by the natives *nullahs*. These abounded with fish which the people took in the following singular manner. They inclosed certain spaces of the water in pools by walls of stones. Into these pools they threw the bruised roots of a plant possessing a soporific quality. These infected the water to such a degree as to stupify the fish, which rose at once to the surface and were taken by the hand.

5. After travelling seventeen days among the mountains, Captain Hardwicke reached Serinagur, the capital of the country. It was by no means agreeably situated, but this was the only spot throughout the whole range of territory where a town could be built.

6. It is related that when the Sultan Akbar was fixing the revenue of his empire, he ordered the Rajah of Serinagur to bring him a map of his country. The Rajah went out and brought in a lean camel, saying, "My territory is like this beast, all up and down, scraggy, lean and bare." The sultan was so amused with the aptness of the illustration, and so impressed with the picture which it represented of the poverty of the country, that he remitted the Rajah's tribute, altogether.

7. Captain Hardwicke was unable to proceed any farther than Serinagur, and a second company of travellers, comprising Mr. Colebrooke and Captains Raper, Hearsey and Webb, were sent in the same direction in 1808. They went over the craggy mountains by the most fearful passes, which ran along the edges of precipices where a single mis-step would have plunged them into abysses thousands of feet deep. The natives,

---

3. What did he find at Haridwar? 4. What are *nullahs*? How are fish taken in them? 5. Describe Serinagur. 6. What anecdote is related of the Rajah? 7. Describe the mountain journey.

however, leaped along these dangerous paths with the most fearless agility.

8. On ascending a high mountain, they came to a small table-land at its summit, the prospect from which presented a scene so grand that imagination could never go beyond it. From the top to the bottom was a perpendicular height of at least four thousand feet: while above, seven or eight chains of mountains successively rose behind each other till the view was bounded by the snowy pinnacles of the mighty Himmaleh.

9. The almost unfathomable depth of the valley beneath, contrasted with the stupendous height of the mountains above, and the grandeur of their awful and cloud-capt boundary, produced an impression of sublimity amounting almost to terror. Farther up the mountains was a place called Gangoutri, and in this neighborhood the natives assured them the Ganges first made its appearance, issuing from something to which they gave the name of the "Cow's Mouth."

10. The travellers attempted to ascend to this place, but they found the labor so enormous by reason of steep ascents, immense rocks, loose stones, and furious mountain-torrents, that they were forced to desist. But being determined to learn as much as possible of the place in question, they sent forward four Hindoos of their company, who were more accustomed to encounter such obstacles.

11. These natives, after three weeks' absence, returned with a most fearful account of their adventures and hair-breadth escapes. They were particularly dismayed by a storm of snow, an object which they had never seen before. They traced the river to a spot where it was entirely covered with beds of snow, which no one had yet been able to penetrate. The Cow's Mouth was a rock in the river partly appearing above the water in a shape which the fancy of the Hindoos had converted into a representation of the jaws of a cow.

---

8. A scene in the mountains. 9. Gangoutri. 10. The obstacles encountered by the travellers. 11. What is the Cow's Mouth?

CHAPTER LXXXIII.

THE BRITISH EMBASSY TO PERSIA.

King of Persia.

1. In 1801 the British government sent Colonel Malcolm on an embassy to Persia, with a view to gain the alliance of that power against the French. This undertaking was successful. Futeh Ali Shah, the sovereign of Persia, made a treaty with Great Britain, which, according to the terms of it, was to be binding on himself and his posterity as long as the world should exist. By this treaty all Frenchmen were prohibited from entering Persia on pain of death.

CHAPTER LXXXIII.— *Questions.*— 1. When did Colonel Malcolm go to Persia? What treaty did he make?

2. But a very few years had elapsed when the British heard that notwithstanding the stipulations of this everlasting treaty, a French agent had been allowed to settle at the Persian court, where he enjoyed the highest power, and was employed in disciplining the troops after the European manner. In 1808 it appeared that the shah had sent an embassy to Paris.

3. In fact, Napoleon, whose mind was intent on foreign conquest, courted this oriental potentate partly as an auxiliary against Russia, and partly perhaps with a remote view to some future operations against British India. He returned the embassy of Futeh Ali by a very splendid one under General Gardenne, which obtained a distinguished reception, and gained the entire confidence of the Persian court.

4. The British government determined to counteract this proceeding, and accordingly dispatched Sir Harford Jones on an embassy to the shah. He landed at Bushire on the Persian Gulf, and proceeded to Shiraz and Persepolis. At the latter place the English discovered the ancient palace of Sapor which had escaped the researches of former travellers.

5. The view of Ispahan from the distance of five miles, with its palaces, spires, and beautiful environs, appeared to them one of the most magnificent prospects in the world, and conveying no tidings of the misfortunes which this celebrated city had suffered. When they entered it, however, the prospect was reversed. The walls were levelled with the ground, the vast suburbs were almost deserted, and a traveller might have ridden about it for miles without meeting anything but ruins.

6. From Ispahan the embassy proceeded to Teheran, the present capital of Persia. It is situated near the northern frontier, and is convenient for war against Russia now the most threatening foe of Persia. The reception of the embassy from the time of its entrance into Persia had been very favorable. Sir Harford made a skilful display of that magnificence which is peculiarly calculated to dazzle the eyes of the orientals.

---

2. How was it observed? 3. What was done by Napoleon? 4. What is said of the embassy of Sir Harford Jones? What of Persepolis? 5. Of Ispahan? 6, 7. What took place at Teheran?

7. At Teheran the Persian minister waited upon him, attended by the royal poet. A great part of the conversation consisted in loading this personage with the most extravagant praises. All agreed that he was the greatest bard of the age. The shah gave him a gold *tomaur*, upwards of five dollars, for every couplet he wrote.

8. At the audience with the shah, the ambassador began to negotiate the terms of a proposed treaty. This negotiation was conducted in a manner very different from our ideas of decorum. The discussions sometimes led to violent quarrels, and at other times were interrupted by loud bursts of laughter. Once, in the midst of the most serious deliberation, the Persian minister broke off by asking the ambassador to relate the history of the world from the creation. This man must have had a love for long stories, indeed.

9. Afterwards, when the minister had promised to send a copy of the treaty fully written out, the ambassador received instead of it a large citron. When the treaty was at length produced, the secretary, who valued himself on being the finest writer in Persia, had so filled it with oriental flourishes and conceits, that it no longer retained any intelligible meaning. He was compelled, much against his will, to reduce it to a form more suited to a European understanding.

10. When the minister came finally to apply the seals, he cried out, "Strike! strike!" while all the Persians present exclaimed, "God grant the friendship between the two nations may be lasting! God grant it! God grant it!" Irregularly as this negotiation had been conducted, its result was completely successful to the English. They obtained all their demands, while Gardenne received his dismissal, being prohibited at the same time to go by the way of Georgia, lest he should hold communication with the Russians. Persia remained from this time entirely subjected to British influence.

---

8. What of the audience with the shah? How did the Persian minister behave? 9. How the secretary? 10. What took place at the sealing of the treaty? What was the result of it?

CHAPTER LXXXIV.

MOORCROFT'S TRAVELS TO THIBET.

1. No other European traveller has penetrated so far into a mountainous part of India as Mr. Moorcroft. In the year 1819 he undertook a journey to Thibet with a view of procuring some of the goats that furnish the hair from which the celebrated cashmere shawls are manufactured. He hired a Hindoo Pundit to be the companion of his journey; and in order to measure accurately the distance traversed, it was stipulated in the bargain that the Pundit should make every stride in walking exactly four feet in length!

2. Strange as it may seem, this condition was faithfully observed, notwithstanding their route often lay through the most rugged and uneven country, where it required the nicest selection to find a spot on which the feet could be placed with safety. Every day the Pundit wrote down carefully the number of steps he had taken.

3. The journey was full of dangers. The travellers proceeded along the broken and perpendicular sides of tremendous cliffs where vast masses of rock frequently poured down in broken fragments, burying all the roads, tracks and bridges beneath. Sometimes a whole forest slid off the face of a hill, with the earth on which it stood, and precipitated itself into the valley beneath, where the trees lay with their roots uppermost.

4. Mr. Moorcroft was once awakened by a crashing sound, and looking out saw a shower of stones descending from the heights above him, several of which rushed by him with a force almost equal to that of a cannon-ball. After a week's travel through parts like these, he came to a little village called *Malari*, situated in the corner of a triangular valley shut in by lofty mountains.

CHAPTER LXXXIV. *Questions.*—1. When did Mr. Moorcroft travel? What was his object? 2. What strange bargain did he make with a Pundit? 3. Describe the journey. Its dangers. 4. What adventure happened to Mr. Moorcroft?

5. The houses contained neither lock nor bolt, but to the outer door of each was fastened a rope, and to the end of this a large dog, who acted the part of a vigilant guardian. The inhabitants were of a mixed Tartar and Hindoo race, and the walls of their houses were ornamented with flowers, and figures of Hindoo deities. They traded between Thibet and Serinagur, conveying borax and salt on the backs of goats and sheep.

6. Two days' travel beyond this place brought Mr. Moorcroft and his companions to Niti, on the extreme north-eastern frontier of Hindostan. There they found the changes of heat and cold most remarkable. In the morning four coats were hardly enough to make them comfortable, but as day advanced, it was necessary to throw off one after another till at length a thick dress became unsupportable. After three o'clock a reverse process began, and coat after coat was put on till the whole were resumed.

7. As they continued to ascend the mountains they found it very difficult to breathe, and at every three or four steps they were compelled to stop and gasp for breath. In attempting to sleep, this difficulty of breathing became more painful than ever. Sometimes Mr. Moorcroft's whole frame was affected, and he felt a giddiness in the head which appeared to threaten apoplexy. His hands, neck and face grew very red, the skin sore, and blood burst from his lips.

8. Having made his way safely across the mountains, he descended into Thibet and reached the town of Daba, the residence of a Lama. This person lived with his *Gelums* or monks in a monastery in the centre of the town, which contained many temples of a circular shape, diminishing by smaller circles upward, and terminating in an umbrella-shaped copper roof with a gilded pinnacle. The grand temple was painted red, and decorated with horns and grotesque figures. In one of the rooms was a large number of leather masks imitating the faces of wild beasts and demons. These were designed to be used at some great festival.

---

5. Describe Malari. 6. What is said of the heat and cold at Niti? 7. Of the difficulty of breathing on the mountains? 8. What is said of Daba and the Lama?

9. The Lama behaved very courteously to Mr. Moorcroft and his companions. At parting, he took hold of one of their gowns and said in a very affecting tone, "I pray you let me live in your recollection as white as this cloth." The *Gelums* appeared to be a dirty, greasy, good-humored, happy set of fellows, who in spite of their sacred vocation carried on considerable trade.

10. Penetrating still farther into the interior, Mr. Moorcroft arrived at the lake of Mavasarowara, a sacred and celebrated body of water, the object of religious veneration throughout Hindostan, and which is believed to be the source of its most famous rivers. The scene here was magnificent. The lake was surrounded by tremendous craggy mountains, above which rose the loftiest summits of the Himmaleh clad in perpetual snow.

11. Of all the holy places revered by a people devoted to pilgrimage, none can rival this lake. Once to behold the waters of the Mavasarowara is regarded by the Hindoos as a felicity beyond every other on earth. The cliffs on its borders for a circuit of twenty or thirty miles are studded with convents full of recluses.

12. Mr. Moorcroft, although he succeeded in penetrating farther into this country than any traveller who had preceded him, yet was not fortunate enough to obtain any of the Thibet goats. He returned to the British territory in India after further perils and hair-breadth escapes. The favorable reception given to him by the authorities of Thibet excited the highest indignation in the Chinese government, which holds sway over this country.

13. The magistrate who had befriended Mr. Moorcroft was deprived of his office, and orders were given to prohibit all the attempts of the English to enter the country. Lieutenant Webb, in endeavoring to follow in the footsteps of Mr. Moorcroft, was stopped at the frontier, and assured that none of his countrymen would thenceforth be permitted to cross the mountains.

---

9. How did the Lama behave? Describe the *Gelums*. 10. The lake of Mavasarowara. 12. What was the success of Mr. Moorcroft's journey? 13. What was the conduct of the Chinese government?

CHAPTER LXXXV.

PALESTINE—AMERICAN EXPEDITION TO THE DEAD SEA.

1. In the year 1847 the United States government dispatched an expedition to Palestine, for the purpose of making researches in and around the Dead Sea. This remarkable body of water has been an object of curiosity to the world from the remotest antiquity. The ancient historians, as well as modern travellers, give such descriptions as rather excite than gratify our curiosity. We have already noticed this subject, but it is worthy of a more detailed account.

2. The bed of this sea was once dry land, and was called the Vale of Siddim. The cities of Sodom, Gomorrah, with others, were situated here, but these were destroyed by a fiery eruption which is supposed to have been of a volcanic nature, in the time of the patriarch Abraham. Ever since this catastrophe the spot has been occupied by a lake of exceedingly salt and bitter water, abounding with bitumen. The neighborhood of the Dead Sea is a barren desert, exposed to the inroads of the wild Bedouin Arabs, in consequence of which few travellers have ventured to risk their lives in that quarter.

3. The exploring party appointed by the American government embarked in the *Supply*, a small ship of war or store-ship, under the command of Lieutenant Lynch. They sailed from New York in November 1847, and on the 15th of February following arrived at Smyrna. Here Lieutenant Lynch left his ship, and went in an Austrian steamboat to Constantinople, for the purpose of getting permission of the Turkish government to make the proposed exploration in Palestine. Such a permission is called by the Turks a *firman*, and

---

Chapter LXXXV.—*Questions.*—1. When was the United States expedition sent to Palestine? What is said of the Dead Sea? 2. What catastrophe happened here? What is its present condition? 3. Describe the outset of the expedition. What is a *firman*?

Lieutenant Lynch waited upon the Sultan to make application for it.

4. He was conducted through various apartments and galleries of the palace, filled with Turkish officers, who sat gravely smoking their pipes, and at last came to a hall most gorgeously furnished with rich carpets, splendid divans, and tables. A magnificent chandelier, all crystal and gold, hung from the ceiling, and at one end of the hall was suspended a crimson velvet curtain embroidered and fringed with gold. Behind this curtain sat the Sultan.

5. He received the Lieutenant with civility. The latter presented him in the name of the President of the United States with some books and prints describing the North American Indians. The Sultan examined them and complimented the Americans on their progress in civilization. The *firman* was granted, and the Sultan behaved throughout in the politest manner.

6. Lieutenant Lynch then returned to Smyrna, and sailed in the Supply to Beyrout in Syria, and from thence to St. John d'Acre, in Palestine, where the expedition began their march inland. They carried tents to encamp in, and two small boats called the Fanny Mason and Fanny Skinner, which were designed for the navigation of the Dead Sea. Crowds of ragged Arabs collected round them at their outset. These stole the copper thole-pins from the boats, imagining they were gold. The Yankee sailors drove away the thieves at the point of the bayonet.

7. Before the expedition was well on its way, the Turkish governor came to the Lieutenant with an alarming story of the hostile Arabs on the banks of the Jordan, who, he said, would assuredly rob and murder every man who fell into their hands. He was of opinion that the expedition could not proceed in safety without a guard of one hundred soldiers, which he was willing to supply for 20,000 piastres, or about 800 dollars.

8. The Americans knew this was only a trick to ex-

4, 5. Describe the interview with the Sultan. 6. How did the Arabs behave to the Americans? 7. What was the conduct of the Turkish governor. 8. How did Lieutenant Lynch reply to him?

tort money, and they laughed at him. Lieutenant Lynch showed him his revolvers, and a sword with pistol barrels attached to the hilt. The governor said it was "the devil's invention." The Lieutenant told him, "we have fifteen men with many of these swords and pistols, one great gun, a blunderbuss, a rifle, fourteen carbines with bayonets, and twelve bowie-knife pistols—Do you not think we can go down the Jordan?" The governor replied, "You will, if any can." The Americans thought the same, and marched onward.

9. Sometimes the Arabs hung about them apparently watching a favorable moment for robbing them, but a vigilant watch was kept by the travellers, and the expedition reached the Sea of Galilee in safety. The hills round it were covered with corn-fields and flower-gardens. Ragged peasants were ploughing in the fields, but not a tree nor house was to be seen. By the side of a fountain on the road side from Jerusalem to Damascus, they saw a company of Christian pilgrims with their horses waiting their turn to drink. At a distance beyond the sea were the mountains of Bashan.

10. At the town of Tiberias, on the banks of the lake, the Americans obtained accommodations from the chief rabbi of the Jews. They launched their two boats and hoisted the American flag for the first time in the world, upon the Sea of Galilee. Another boat was purchased of the natives, and named the "Uncle Sam." This little fleet sailed along the coast, while the remainder of the expedition proceeded by land.

11. They passed many rivers, and at length came to the spot where the river Jordan runs out of the lake. Here they encamped. They had two American tents, one Arab, and one Egyptian, of many different colors—white, green, blue and crimson. In the soft and mellow light of the moon the scene was very beautiful.

12. Many wild and savage-looking Arabs were found dwelling on the banks of the Jordan, but they did not molest the travellers. A very strict watch was kept by the Americans. Every one lay down to sleep with his arms beside him and his cartridge belt on. Watchfires

---

9. What is said of the Sea of Galilee? 10. What of the American boats? 11. The tents? 12. The Arabs?

were kept burning, and their light often shone on the ruins of villages where the peasant had been driven from his home by the Bedouin robbers.

13. As they proceeded down the stream, they met with many obstacles from the rocks, and at length the Uncle Sam foundered. The other boats being made of copper, survived these dangers. Fields of wheat and barley were seen around, without a human being, or a tent, or hut in sight of them.

CHAPTER LXXXVI.

THE BEDOUIN ARABS—THE DEAD SEA.

1. At length they came in sight of an encampment of black tents, and several Arabs advanced to meet them, bearing a tufted spear which is a symbol of the presence of the sheik. The Americans entered one of the tents, where they were regaled with coffee and pipes. Little naked Arab boys and girls were tumbling about in the grass. The tents were thirty or forty in number, and made of coarse goats-hair cloth. The Arabs entertained their visitors with boiled rice and butter, which is the common food of these people.

2. Many encampments of this sort were met in the passage down the Jordan, and the Arabs everywhere crowded round the travellers with the greatest curiosity. Near Jericho they met a great crowd of pilgrims. It was before daylight in the morning, and the Americans were sleeping quietly in their tents, when they were aroused by the intelligence of the approach of a disorderly troop of strangers. Rising in haste, they beheld thousands of torchlights with a dark mass beneath, moving rapidly over the hills. They struck their tents with precipitation, and removed out of the way.

3. A few moments after, the whole crowd of pilgrims rushed by, men, women, and children, mounted on ca-

---

13. The country?
CHAPTER LXXXVI. —*Questions.*—1. What is said of an Arab encampment? 2. What did the party meet near Jericho? 3, 4. Describe the pilgrims.

mels, horses, mules and donkeys, in a tumultuous mass, like the fugitives of a routed army. The Americans would have been trampled under foot, but for their friends, the Bedouin Arabs, who mounted their steeds and formed a line round them. But this was only the advanced guard of a great army of pilgrims, who about two hours afterward, just as the day was dawning, made their appearance on the crest of a high ridge, in one tumultuous throng.

4. They were all hurrying toward the Jordan in the wild haste of a disorderly rout. People of all nations were mixed together, Syrians, Egyptians, Armenians, Russians, Poles, and persons from almost every part of Europe, Asia, and even America. Men, women, and children of every age and hue, and in every variety of dress, talking, screaming and shouting in all languages. Many of the women and children were suspended in baskets and cages from the backs of camels, donkeys, and horses. All eyes were stretched toward the Jordan, and heedless of all obstacles, they hurried eagerly forward, dismounted and stripped off their clothes, rushed down the bank and threw themselves into the stream.

5. Each one plunged himself or was dipped by another three times below the surface, in honor of the Trinity, and then filled a bottle with the water. Many of them cut branches from the trees on the banks, dipped them in the water, and bore them away as memorials of their visit. The number of pilgrims was estimated at eight thousand.

6. When the Americans reached the Dead Sea, they found it to present a dismal spectacle. The banks were desolate. The mountains surrounding it seemed like iron. The water of the sea was of so sharp a saltness, that it caused a prickly sensation wherever it touched the skin. The scene around was one of unmixed desolation. The air was tainted with sulphurous exhalations. No vegetation was to be seen; nothing met the view but barren mountains, fragments of rocks blackened by sulphur, and a sea of dark and heavy waters, with a few dead trees upon its margin.

---

5. How did they behave in the Jordan? 6. How did the Dead Sea look?

Pillar of Salt.

7. The boats coasted along and made examination as to the depth of the water, the nature of the soil on the banks, &c. At a place called Usdum, which is supposed to be the same with ancient Sodom, they saw a great rock called Lot's Wife. This is a lofty, round pillar of solid salt, capped with limestone. The upper or rounded part is about forty feet high; this rests on a sort of oval pedestal about sixty feet above the level of the sea. This is, doubtless, the pillar mentioned by Josephus, who says, "Lot's wife was changed into a pillar of salt which remains to this day, for I have seen it." Some of the early Christian writers also mention this curiosity.

8. No fish of any sort were found in the waters of the Dead Sea. A large body of wild Arabs came up to the American party, brandishing their lances, clubs and

---

7. What is said of Lot's Wife? 8. What is said of the wild Arabs?

guns. Lieutenant Lynch advanced to meet them, and drew a line upon the ground, telling them if they crossed it they would be fired upon. This intimidated them, and instead of robbing, they fell to begging. Some food and tobacco were given to them, which they chose to accept, peaceably, rather than run the hazard of encountering American rifles.

9. The expedition, after having ascertained that there was no further discovery of great interest to be made in the Dead Sea, bade adieu to those gloomy waters, and took the rout to Jerusalem. They made explorations in the city and the neighborhood, which gave occasion to the inhabitants to say, "The Franks are preparing to take possession of the Holy City." On their approach to a village in which were the ruins of a Christian Church, an old Arab cried out, "O ye Mahometans! come forth and see the Christians searching for treasure concealed by their forefathers in this country."

10. During the latter part of the journey, many of the travellers were taken ill with a peculiar disease which seems to have attacked almost every one who has ventured to explore the banks of the Dead Sea, and which is probably occasioned by the noxious exhalations which arise from its waters. On their return to Beyrout, one of them died. The party were compelled to leave this place speedily, as the physicians assured them there could be no hope of their recovering as long as they remained there. They accordingly embarked at Beyrout, and in December, 1848, arrived in the United States.

---

9. What happened to the Americans on their return?
10. What at Beyrout?

OCEANICA.*

CHAPTER LXXXVII.

MALAYSIA.

MALAYS.

1. UNDER the term *Malaysia*, are comprehended those East India islands inhabited by the genuine Malay tribes, as Java, Borneo, Celebes, and others in their neighborhood. Some of these islands have also other races of men dwelling in them, but the Malays are the

---

* Oceanica consists of the numerous groups of islands in the Pacific Ocean.

It is divided into the *Asiatic Islands*, or *Malaysia, Australasia*, and *Polynesia*. Most of these are within the tropics, and have warm climates. Many are exceedingly prolific, yielding rich

---

CHAPTER LXXXVII.—*Questions.*—1. Describe Malaysia.

MALAYSIA.

most important, and give these islands their prominent characteristics. The peninsula of Malacca is also regarded by some as coming within the division of Malaysia. The islands are often called the Indian Archipelago.

2. *Java*, the most important of these, is six hundred miles in length, and very populous and fertile. From whence came its first inhabitants, it is impossible to say, as the early history of the island is completely lost. There are remains of ancient temples, palaces, and royal

---

spices and various fruits. The natives of these are mostly in a barbarous state.

Malaysia contains several important and fruitful islands, mostly under European governments, as follows:

Names.	Possessed by	Extent.	Pop.	Chief Towns.
Sunda Islands.				
Sumatra	Natives	180,000	4,500,000	Bencoolen.
Java	Dutch	52,000	4,280,000	Batavia.
Banca	Dutch	5,600	80,000	
Timor	Dutch and Portuguese	8,800	100,000	Lifas
Moluccas.				
Amboyna	Dutch	450	45,000	Amboyna.
Ceram	Dutch	4,000	120,000	
Gilolo	Dutch	12,000		Santanag.
Banda Islands	Dutch			
Borneo	Natives	300,000	3,500,000	Borneo.
Celebes	Dutch	75,000	2,500,000	Macassar.
Philippine Isles.				
Luzon	Spaniards	70,000	1,200,000	Manilla.
Mindanao	Spaniards	30,000	900,000	Mindanao.
Samar	Spaniards	800	84,000	
Negros	Spaniards	500	75,000	

Australasia contains the following:

Names.	Square miles.	White Pop.	Native Pop.	Total Pop.
New Holland	3,000,000	110,000	60,000	170,000
Van Dieman's Land	12,209	50,000	3,000	53,000
New Caledonia	6,108		40,000	40,000
New Hebrides	2,291		150,000	150,000
Queen Charlotte's Island	1,537		30,000	30,000
Solomon's Isles	17,610		100,000	100,000
Louisiades	764		10,000	10,000
New Britain	24,433		65,000	65,000
New Guinea	305,540		500,000	500,000
New Zealand			250,000	250,000
		160,000	1,208,000	1,368,000

Polynesia comprises the numerous groups of islands lying to the east of Malaysia and Australasia.

Among these groups, the principal are the *Ladrones, Caro-*

---

2. Java. Its early history, antiquities, &c.

tombs, numerous statues of stone and brass, with engraved inscriptions, which at this day point out the capital cities and towns of native states.

3. The inhabitants were pagans and idolaters till the fifteenth century, though many Mahometan emigrants from the continent of India had settled among them. At length about the year 1470, these emigrants were sufficiently numerous to effect a political and religious revolution in the island. Many of them were persons who had travelled and become familiar with the manners of other nations; all were superior in intelligence to the native Javanese, and were therefore capable of acting, in combination, for a great end.

4. These men were actuated by a religious zeal, and at length found an ambitious, persevering and able leader, under whose guidance they overthrew the native princes and made themselves masters of the country. Having subdued it, the next work of the conquerors was to propagate the Mahometan religion, which proved to be no difficult task, as the paganism of the aborigines was a religion which never took strong hold of the imagination, and was already on the decline.

5. The most active and distinguished of the leaders in the work of conversion are known by the name of the nine *Susuhunans*, or apostles, of whom as many fabulous and

---

line, *Mulgrave, Friendly, Society, Marquesas,* and *Sandwich Isles.* Most of them are fruitful, and yield the bread-fruit, plantain, banana, cocoanut, with citrons, oranges, pine-apples, and other tropical productions. The natives are of the Malay race, though rendered gentle by a soft climate.

The Sandwich Islands are particularly interesting, as the people have been converted to Christianity and civilization by the American missionaries. Honolulu, on the Island of Oahu, is the capital, and contains six thousand inhabitants, mostly natives. On these islands are churches, books, newspapers, magazines, and printing-offices; and in the port of the capital, foreign vessels are always to be seen.

---

3. What is said of the ancient inhabitants? Of the emigrants to Java? 4. What revolution did they effect? What religion did they introduce? 5. What were the *Susuhunans?* What was probably their real character? What is said of the Javanese sultans?

puerile tales are related as of the European monks in the dark ages. They seem to have been a body of adventurers who traded in religion as well as merchandise, and were remarkably characterized by the petty cunning which belongs to travelling pedlars. The Javanese sultans were generally tyrannical and unscrupulous in shedding blood. Their history is little more than a series of wars, massacres, and assassinations.

6. The Portuguese were the first Christian nation that formed settlements in this island, but they were expelled by the Dutch, as we have related elsewhere. The Dutch now hold the sovereignty of Java, though many of the native princes exercise an almost independent sway within their own limits, or merely paying tribute and homage to the Dutch government.

CHAPTER LXXXVIII.

CELEBES—ITS LEGENDS.

1. CELEBES is a large island of a very irregular shape. The two most important tribes inhabiting it are called Macassars and Bugis; their history is quite as uncertain as that of the Javanese. The Macassars have a tradition to the following effect. On a certain time, after the death of four kings, a beautiful woman adorned with a chain of gold, descended from heaven and was acknowledged by the Macassars for their queen, under the name of *Tocmanoerong* — which signifies one descended from heaven.

2. The king of Bantam, in Java, heard the report of the descent on earth of this celestial beauty, and immediately went to Celebes to demand her in marriage, although he had already a wife. His suit was granted, and by this celestial spouse he had a son of such surprising qualities, that he could both talk and walk as soon

---

6. What of the Portuguese and Dutch?
CHAPTER LXXXVIII.—*Questions.*—1. Describe Celebes. Its inhabitants. What tradition have the Macassars? 2. What was done by the king of Bantam? What is said of his son?

as he was born; but he was very much deformed in shape.

3. When he grew up, he broke the gold chain which his mother had brought from heaven, in consequence of which she immediately vanished into the clouds in company with her husband, taking with her one half of the chain, and leaving the other half and the empire to her son. The Macassars pretend that this chain was long preserved by their kings among the royal ornaments, till at length it disappeared, nobody knows how.

4. The history of these people contains hardly anything but perpetual wars and petty conquests, with constant anarchy and violence. The very names of the sovereigns indicate the turbulence and disorder which characterized the state of society in the island. In the native records of Celebes, the princes are usually designated by the circumstances in which they died. The uncertain and wandering life which they led, and the want of a fixed residence, must have given rise to the practice of naming them from the place of their death.

5. One prince is called the *Throat-cutter;* another, *He who ran a muck;* another, *He who had his head cut off;* another, *He who was beaten to death on his own stair-case.* One of them is described as a cannibal who was remarkably fond of human flesh. It is said that he fattened his prisoners for the table, and cutting their hearts out, ate them raw, with pepper and salt! Mahometanism was introduced into Celebes in the early part of the seventeenth century. The Portuguese and Dutch were rivals for the supremacy here, but the Dutch finally prevailed.

---

3. What became of his father and mother and the gold chain? 4. What is said of the history of these people? 5. What names were given to their princes? What atrocities are related of one of them?

CHAPTER LXXXIX.

BORNEO AND THE PHILIPPINES.

1. BORNEO, although the largest island of the East Indian Archipelago, yet can scarcely be said to have a history. It has no deep bays or inlets to facilitate commerce, and has therefore been little visited by strangers. Many settlements of Malays are established on the coast. The interior is inhabited by an aboriginal negro race, called *Dyaks*, who are described as a people of very barbarous manners.

2. The Malay princes call themselves Sultans, and observe great state in their ceremonies. One of these chiefs has conferred the title of *Rajah* or prince on Sir James Brooke, an Englishman who has formed a settlement on the western coast, near the small island of Labuan, which bids fair to become a place of commercial importance.

3. The PHILIPPINE ISLANDS were discovered in 1521, by Magellan, a Portuguese navigator, who sailed on a voyage of discovery in the Spanish service. He passed through the straits which bear his name, and was the first European who sailed across the Pacific Ocean. He met with only two small islands in this passage, till he reached the great cluster of the Philippines.

4. Here he was hospitably received by the inhabitants of Mindanao. At another island called Zebu, he also met with a friendly welcome, and was regarded by the natives as a person sent from heaven. But Magellan, though a man of genius, was deficient in prudence and moderation, and was moreover strongly tinctured with that indiscreet religious zeal which was the characteristic vice of his age.

5. He was seized with an ardent desire to convert the islanders to Christianity, and was unwise enough to

---

CHAPTER LXXXIX.—*Questions.*—1. Describe Borneo. Its inhabitants. 2. What is said of the Malay sultans? Of Sir James Brooke? 3. Who discovered the Philippines? 4. How was Magellan received in these islands? What was his character? 5. How did he attempt to convert the natives of Zebu?

suppose this might be done at the expense of a few ceremonies. He accordingly set up a cross in Zebu, and sprinkled a little water on the king and some of his subjects. Having done this, he supposed he had established Christianity forever in the island.

6. But his efforts led to a result very different from what he expected. The petty prince of the little island of Mactan, which lies opposite Zebu, happened to be a man endowed with a strength of mind above the fears of his countrymen. He perceived that the Spaniards were not celestial beings, but were mortal men. He challenged Magellan to meet him in combat, and the hardy adventurer, with the characteristic chivalry of his time, accepted the challenge.

7. Fifty Spaniards in armor marched to battle against a host of islanders. They were decoyed into a marsh where they were compelled to fight up to their necks in water. Magellan was killed, with six of his companions. The rest saved themselves by a precipitate flight.

8. The people of Zebu were now convinced that their visitors were men, and they soon began to suspect that they were dangerous invaders. The king devised treacherous schemes to cut them off, but the Spaniards escaped from the island, and after visiting various others in this quarter, returned to Spain.

CHAPTER XC.

AUSTRALASIA—NEW HOLLAND—VAN DIEMAN'S LAND.

1. AUSTRALIA or NEW HOLLAND is by some geographers termed a continent, and by others, the largest island in the world. It is about 8,000 miles in circuit. Little is known of the interior, but it appears to be very

---

6. What was done by a neighboring prince? 7. What then took place? What became of Magellan? 8. What of his companions?

CHAPTER XCI.—*Questions.*—1. Describe New Holland. Its inhabitants.

deficient in rivers. The whole territory is dry, and better adapted to pasturing sheep and cattle than to agriculture. The native inhabitants are negroes in the lowest state of savage life. They have little but the gift of speech to raise them above the rank of orang-outangs.

2. The Spaniards and Portuguese were the first discoverers of this part of the world, though the date of this event cannot be precisely fixed. The Dutch afterwards made discoveries here, and called the country New Holland. In 1777, Captain Cook visited the eastern coast, and took possession of it in the name of the king of England. He named this part of the country New South Wales.

3. In 1788, the British government determined to send their convicted felons to this quarter. They accordingly established a colony at Port Jackson, near Botany Bay. From this point, the settlements have extended in every quarter, till at the present day, Australia has become an important part of the British colonial empire.

4. VAN DIEMAN'S LAND was at first supposed to be a part of New Holland, but it was afterwards found to be a separate island. The first settlement was made here in 1803, since which time the colonization of the island has rapidly increased. The natives are of the same general character with those of New Holland, or, if possible, still more barbarous. They cannot even catch a fish, or make a canoe to cross a river, but know only enough to put together a miserable sort of raft when they have a stream of water to pass.

5. NEW GUINEA or PAPUA is a very large island near New Holland, but it has been so little explored by voyagers, that the greater part is less known to us than the interior of Africa or Asia. From what has been seen of it, this island appears to be one of the finest spots of territory on the face of the globe. The few navigators who have sailed along the coast have observed ranges of mountains swelling up behind each other, their summits rising in the most picturesque and varied forms and clothed with immense pine forests.

---

2. By whom was it discovered? 3. When were settlements made here? 4. Describe Van Dieman's Land. Its inhabitants. 5. Describe New Guinea. How much of it is known?

6. The inhabitants of New Guinea are negroes of very ferocious manners, but more civilized than the New Hollanders. The Malays of Borneo and Celebes frequently land here and carry away the natives for slaves. This has rendered them hostile to all strangers, so that the voyagers who touch upon the coast are compelled to be carefully on their guard. There is no European settlement in New Guinea, except a small one established by the Dutch in 1828, at Turan Bay.

CHAPTER XCI.

NEW ZEALAND.

1. To the southwest of New Holland, and forming a part of Australasia, is a group of islands, of a very interesting character.

2. NEW ZEALAND is the name given to the two largest of these. They lie close to each other, sepa-

---

6. What is said of its inhabitants? What European settlement is here?

CHAPTER XCI. — *Questions.* — 2. Describe New Zealand. Who discovered it?

rated by a narrow strait, in the southern part of the Pacific. The Dutch navigator, Zasman, first discovered them in 1642, and they were supposed to form a single island till 1769, when Captain Cook sailed through the strait which divides them, and gave it his own name.

3. But the Dutch and the English found the natives fierce and inhospitable. Captain Cook's men, in a quarrel, killed four of them, but the islanders fought with great bravery. A little afterwards, a French ship touching here, was received with kindness, but the commander treacherously repaid this hospitality by seizing and carrying off one of the chiefs.

4. Three years afterwards, the New Zealanders avenged themselves. Another French vessel arriving here, the natives inveigled them on shore by a show of confidence, and captured twenty-seven of their officers and crew, whom they killed and devoured. In 1773, ten more Frenchmen met with the same fate. After this, the New Zealanders became less hostile to strangers, and were visited by many ships, with the crews of which they carried on a friendly intercourse.

5. But in 1809, they committed another terrible massacre upon a very slight provocation, slaughtering a whole ship's crew of nearly seventy persons. Notwithstanding this discouraging calamity, the endeavors of the Europeans to maintain an intercourse with the natives were persevered in, and at length their enmity was so far subdued that the English formed settlements in the country.

6. These settlements have rapidly augmented of late years, and New Zealand is now one of the most important of the British colonies, receiving yearly large numbers of emigrants from the mother country. The American whale ships also resort to these islands for supplies. Their chief rendezvous is the Bay of Islands.

---

3. How did the natives behave to foreigners? 4. What happened to the French in these islands? 5. What took place in 1809? What afterwards? 6. What is the present condition of New Zealand? Where do the American whale ships resort?

7. The natives of New Zealand, although their country lies near New Holland, are very different from their stupid neighbors. They belong to that Malay race which is spread over the whole of Polynesia. They are tall and well-formed, with large black eyes. They are intelligent, have made some progress in the arts of life, and are united into a certain form of political society.

8. Although they have, at times, shown violent passions, and a sanguinary, revengeful spirit, yet, in their recent intercourse with the British settlers, they appear to be exceedingly gentle and tractable and easily governed. The work of conversion to Christianity goes on rapidly among them, and the odious habits of savages disappear with their gods and idols. Their hitherto uncultivated intellect has been found to be of a high order, and in their commercial dealings, they exhibit a zeal and acuteness which would be remarkable even in Europeans.

CHAPTER XCII.

POLYNESIA—THE SOCIETY ISLANDS—OTAHEITE.

1. THE name of *Polynesia*, signifying "Many Islands," is given to the great mass of islands in the Pacific Ocean. They are mostly small, but are spread over an immense extent of the surface of the globe. According to the belief of some naturalists, they are the fragments of a great continent, which was broken up by some terrible convulsion in the interior of the globe. In general, they are very fertile and covered with vegetation. Some are lofty and mountainous; others are flat, being formed entirely of coral, which is the work of marine insects. The bread-fruit tree, cocoa-nut tree, banana, and other tropical fruits, are found in the Polynesian islands.

---

7. Describe the New Zealand natives. What is their present condition?

CHAPTER XCII.—*Questions.*—1. Describe Polynesia. What theory is entertained of the formation of these islands?

2. The Society Islands, a few years ago, excited a higher interest than any other group in the South Sea, though they are now regarded as less important than the Sandwich group. The Society Islands are not large, but they are the most beautiful and fertile of all the territories of the Pacific.

The Banana Tree.

3. Otaheite, or Tahiti, is the largest and the finest. This island was first discovered by the Spanish navigator Quiros, who gave it the name of *Sagittaria*. It was soon, however, forgotten, and was re-discovered by Captain Wallis, an Englishman. It was first thoroughly explored by Captain Cook, during his first voyage in 1769. The English were enchanted with the beautiful scenery of the island, the fruitfulness of its fields, and the

---

2. Describe the Society Islands. 3. Otaheite. By whom was it discovered? By whom explored? How were the English pleased with it?

The Bread-Fruit Tree.

amiable and engaging manners of its inhabitants. We must add that their morals were, at the same time, very dissolute.

4. The English discoverers did not attempt to form any settlement here, but some years after Cook's visit, the London Missionary Society determined to undertake the conversion of the natives to Christianity. In 1797 a company of missionaries proceeded to Otaheite in the ship Daft commanded by Captain Wilson. They remained ten or twelve years in the island without making a single convert, though the natives treated them well and listened to their sermons. In 1808 most of the missionaries left Otaheite for the neighboring island of Eimeo.

---

4. What was done by the London Missionary Society? How did the missionaries succeed in Otaheite?

OTAHEITE.

5. Shortly after this, an accidental circumstance assisted them in their designs. Pomare, the king of Otaheite, was driven from the island by a rebellion of his subjects and took refuge in Eimeo. In his distress he listened to the exhortations and advice of the missionaries, and became a Christian. Many of the chief men of Eimeo followed his example, and the whole island finally abandoned its ancient superstitions.

6. Pomare was invited back to Otaheite by a body of his adherents. His first attempt was unsuccessful; but in 1815 he completely defeated the Pagan army of the rebels, and regained possession of the whole island. Having done this, he demolished all the temples and altars, and set up the chief idol for a post in his kitchen as a mark of degradation. During his lifetime he supported Christianity, and this policy was continued by his sister Aimata who succeeded him on the throne.

7. The king who succeeded Aimata took an oath of fidelity to the English missionaries on his accession, and was anointed and crowned by them. So lofty was the conception of the missionary character in the minds of the natives, that many of them believed the king of Great Britain was a missionary.

8. The Otaheitans have now spacious churches, in which the natives meet for religious worship decently dressed and with a serious and reverential air. Their religion, however, has still a strong savor of paganism. They pay too much regard to formalities, and they venerate their Bibles in some degree rather as household gods and the means of mysterious protection, than as sources of instruction.

9. Great numbers of the islanders have abandoned their old religion without adopting the new. This class of persons bears the whimsical name of *ouri outi*,

---

5. What happened to Pomare? How did this affect the missionaries? 6. What success had Pomare in recovering Otaheite? What did he do for Christianity? What was done by his sister? 7. What by the successor of Aimata? What idea had the Otaheitans of the missionary character? 8. What is the present state of the Otaheitans? What is the character of their religion? What do they think of the Bible? 9. Who are the *ouri outis?* What is said of the native population?

or "rusty iron." The native population, as in the case of the Sandwich Islands, has much diminished since the arrival of foreigners.

CHAPTER XCIII.

THE SANDWICH ISLANDS—VISIT OF CAPTAIN COOK.

1. These islands lie in the North Pacific Ocean, and have acquired great importance in recent times by the civilization of the inhabitants, and the establishment of European and American settlers among them. They were probably visited by early Spanish navigators, though no written accounts exist of these discoveries. The natives have traditions of these early visitors, and Captain Cook found articles of iron here which had evidently been left by European ships.

2. This navigator first saw the Sandwich Islands in January 1778. The appearance of the ships from the island of Kaui, struck the natives with astonishment. They asked one another, *"What are these great things with branches?"* Some replied, *"It is a forest which has moved into the sea."* This excited in them the greatest consternation.

3. The chiefs sent men in canoes to examine the wondrous machines: they returned and reported that the ships had abundance of iron, which filled the natives with joy, for they prized this metal highly. Those who visited the ships described the Englishmen in this manner. "Their foreheads are white, their eyes are bright; they have rough outsides; their speech is unknown, and their heads are horned like the moon." The natives supposed the hats to be a part of their heads.

Chapter XCIII.—*Questions.*—1. When were the Sandwich Islands first discovered? What did Captain Cook find here? 2. What did the natives say when they saw the ships? 3. What was done by the chiefs? How did the natives describe the English?

VISIT OF CAPTAIN COOK.

4. The report of the great quantity of iron seen on board the ships, excited the cupidity of the chiefs, and one of their warriors volunteered to seize it, saying, "I will go and take it, as it is my business to plunder." He went and in the attempt was fired upon and killed. Notwithstanding this, a friendly intercourse was established with the inhabitants of Kaui, and the news spread to the neighboring islands that strangers had arrived who were gods indeed.

5. It was said they had loose skins, (meaning their clothes,) volcanoes belching fire burned out their mouths, (tobacco pipes,) and in their sides they had doors, (pockets,) which went far into their bodies, into which they thrust their hands and drew out knives, iron, beads, cloth, nails and everything else! When Captain Cook landed on Owhyhee or Hawaii, ten or fifteen thousand men collected to see and worship him, for he was regarded as the chief divinity of the celestial visitants.

6. Heralds announced his approach and opened the way for his progress. A vast throng gathered round him: others more fearful gazed from behind stone walls, from the tree-tops, or from behind the corners of the houses. The moment he approached, they either hid themselves or covered their faces with great apparent awe, while those nearer prostrated themselves on the earth in the deepest humility. As soon as he had passed, all unveiled themselves, rose and followed him.

7. A variety of ceremonies took place, in which Cook was worshipped as a divinity. Afterwards whenever he landed, a priest attended him and regulated the religious ceremonies which were celebrated in his honor. Captain Cook took advantage of this delusion of the natives, and caused the whole island to be taxed to furnish provisions for his ships.

---

4. What happened to a warrior? 5. What story was told of the English in the other islands? 6, 7. How was Captain Cook received on landing at Hawaii?

CHAPTER XCIV.

DEATH OF CAPTAIN COOK.

1. The deception which Captain Cook practised upon the islanders in allowing them to believe him a god, although it was profitable for a time, turned out very unfortunately for him in the end. He first offended the natives by tearing down the wooden work of one of their temples for fuel, and carrying off their idols along with it. The natives then began to quarrel with the crews, and when one of the English died and was brought on shore to be buried, their faith in the divine origin of the strangers was considerably shaken.

2. Captain Cook and his companions had now become common objects among them, and the awe with which they were at first regarded, rapidly diminished. The voracious appetites of the English threatened the islanders with a famine. The crews had arrived lean and hungry, they were now fat and sleek—but yet required daily an enormous supply of provisions. The natives signified by earnest signs to their troublesome visitors, their wishes that they would depart from their island.

3. Cook told them he would sail on a certain day. The glad tidings soon spread, and the rejoicing people at the command of their chief, prepared a farewell present of food, cloth and other articles, which in quantity and value far exceeded anything which they had previously offered. These gifts were all taken on board the ships and nothing given in recompense. It is not surprising that the islanders were in bad humor.

4. The ships sailed, but unfortunately for Captain Cook, his ship sprung her foremast in a gale of wind, which obliged him to return to Hawaii at the end of a

---

Chapter XCIV.—*Questions.*—1. What was the consequence of Captain Cook's deceiving the natives? How did he offend them? 2. How was their regard for him lessened? What is said of the consumption of food by the English? 3. What present did the natives make them? 4. Why did the ships return after leaving the island? How were they received?

DEATH OF CAPTAIN COOK.

week. On approaching the shore the scene presented a striking contrast to that exhibited on the first visit. Instead of seeing the beach thronged with thousands of men, and the waters covered with canoes, they found not a native to bid them welcome.

5. A boat was sent ashore to inquire the cause, and returned with the information that the king was away and had left the bay under a strict *taboo*, which is a sort of religious embargo prohibiting a certain space of territory from being entered by any human being. The fact was that the sudden re-appearance of the ships had alarmed the natives, who were now afraid of being eaten out of house and home by these insatiate guests, who devoured all the productions of their fields, without paying for anything. The islanders were also highly exasperated by the rude and insulting behavior of the English in polluting their sacred places and showing no regard to their religious feelings.

6. Notwithstanding these things, Captain Cook succeeded in renewing his intercourse with the natives, but the latter evinced none of their former cordiality and good will. Quarrels soon arose. A native was killed by a shot from the ships. The English on shore were attacked and driven to their boats by showers of stones, and in the night one of the ship's boats was stolen. Captain Cook went on shore the next day to recover the boat, and was killed by one of the natives, who stabbed him in the back with a dagger.

---

5. What is said of the *taboo*? What alarmed the natives? What exasperated them? 6. How did Captain Cook meet with his death?

CHAPTER XCV.

CIVILIZATION OF THE SANDWICH ISLANDERS.

1. The death of Captain Cook, although occasioned altogether by his own imprudence, caused an unfavorable impression of the character of these islanders to prevail in Europe and America. People, without fully comprehending the causes of that catastrophe, believed the natives to be a cruel race of savages, disposed to commit atrocities upon strangers. The consequence was that for many years no ships ventured to touch upon their shores.

2. After a while they were again visited by English and American vessels, and although some acts of hostility disturbed their intercourse at first, a peaceable traffic was finally established, and both Europeans and Americans settled in the principal islands. In the mean time, the islanders had been making efforts to raise themselves to the level of European arts and civilization.

3. Kamahama, one of their kings, about the year 1794 began to build ships and form a navy. He also

---

Chapter XCV. — *Questions.* — 1. What was the consequence of the death of Capt. Cook? 2. What was done by the English and American vessels? What by the islanders? 3. What by Kamahama? What by Riho Riho?

disciplined a body of troops in the European manner, and erected a fort defended by cannon. His son Riho Riho in 1819 embraced Christianity and abolished idolatrous worship. Through the influence of the American missionaries most of the natives were converted to Christianity.

4. The Sandwich Islands have now a regular government modeled after the fashion of the European monarchies, and a regular code of laws in the native tongue and English, printed at Oahu, for that island has now printing presses, bookstores and newspapers, like a town of the United States. Its chief town Honolulu, is the most thriving commercial mart in Polynesia, and is rapidly augmenting in population. Great numbers of American whale-ships are always to be found in its harbor.

5. But although civilization, traffic and the arts have been introduced into these islands, the native population has much diminished, and there is every reason to believe that the original inhabitants will totally disappear, and be replaced by a population composed chiefly of settlers from the United States and their descendants.

6. The French have made strong efforts to introduce the Catholic religion into these islands, and at one time they had a body of Jesuits busy in attempting to proselyte the natives. But in 1831 they were expelled by the king Kuakini. Within a few years the French have renewed their endeavors to obtain influence in the islands, and their ships of war have committed hostilities here, and attempted to domineer over the government.

7. It is probable, however, that the government of the United States will interfere to protect the islanders in case the French make any serious attempts to subjugate them, as the interests of American commerce require that the neutrality of the Sandwich Islands should be preserved.

---

4. What government exists in the Sandwich Islands? What laws? What is said of Honolulu? 5. What of the native population? 6. What have the French done in these islands? 7. What will the United States probably do?

CHAPTER XCVI.

PITCAIRN'S ISLAND.

1. PITCAIRN'S ISLAND is a very small and solitary spot, situated at a distance from all the large groups in the Pacific; but it is deserving of notice for its singular history. It had no inhabitants previous to its discovery by European ships, but is at present inhabited by a very interesting race of people. The story of its population is as follows.

2. The British government being desirous of cultivating the bread-fruit in the West India islands, despatched, in the year 1789, Captain Bligh in the ship Bounty to Otaheite, to procure a large number of the plants of that tree for this purpose. These were obtained, and the Bounty sailed on her return to the Atlantic. Captain Bligh's tyrannical and oppressive behavior caused a mutiny among his crew, a number of whom, headed by a bold and enterprising man named Christian, took possession of the ship a few days after she had left Otaheite and turned the Captain with a few of the men who remained faithful to him adrift in a boat.

3. Bligh and his companions were now in the middle of the Pacific Ocean, with only a small stock of provisions, and almost entirely destitute of nautical instruments and every article useful in their critical condition. By persevering efforts, however, aided by remarkable good fortune, they reached the island of Timor, near Java, after a voyage of unexampled hazard and suffering. From this place they returned to England in safety.

4. The mutineers in the mean time, steered back to Otaheite, being enchanted with the loveliness and plenty of that beautiful and fertile island, and the amiable

---

CHAPTER XCVI.—*Questions.*— 1. Describe Pitcairn's Island. Its inhabitants. 2. What was the purpose of the voyage of Capt. Bligh? Why did his men mutiny? 3. What did they do with Bligh? How did he and his companions save themselves? 4. What became of the mutineers? Why did they leave Otaheite and Toobooai?

character of the inhabitants. They knew, however, that a long stay here would be dangerous, as ships would be sent from England to search for them. A number of them, therefore, removed to the neighboring island of Toobooai. This was also an unsafe place, as British vessels sometimes were known to touch here.

5. Determining to fix themselves upon some remote and unsuspected spot, they made choice of Pitcairn's Island, and the Bounty sailed for this place in 1790 with Christian and eight others of the mutineers, accompanied by six Otaheitan men and twelve women. They landed on the island, burnt the ship, and took up their abode in this lonely spot.

6. The British frigate Pandora was sent out in pursuit of the mutineers soon after Bligh's return to England. Those of the Bounty's crew who had remained at Otaheite and the neighboring islands, were captured and carried home to England, where some of them were hanged. What became of Christian and his companions was not known till 1809, when a Nantucket whaleship happening to touch at Pitcairn's Island, found this supposed desolate spot to be inhabited by people speaking English.

7. Their story as related by one of them, the only survivor of the Bounty's crew, is this. Not long after their arrival at the island, there arose quarrels among them concerning their wives. These led to bloodshed, and Christian was killed by one of his companions. Others were killed after him, and at the end of ten years only one of the English remained alive.

8. This man's name was Alexander, but he chose to call himself John Adams. He had been a wild and lawless character, but on finding himself left with six women and nineteen children, he became so impressed by thinking on the scenes of crime and misery which he had witnessed that a complete change was wrought in his

---

5. Whom did they take with them to Pitcairn's Island? What became of the Bounty? 6. What is said of the Pandora and the mutineers? When and by whom were the Pitcairn Islanders discovered? 7. What story did they relate of themselves? What became of Christian and the English? 7. Who was the survivor? What change took place in his character? 8. How did he succeed in reforming his companions?

temper and morals. He determined to commence a work of reformation both in himself and in his associates, and this object he fully accomplished.

9. The Otaheitan females proved tractable, and were easily converted. The children were trained up under such instructions as he was able to impart, and became sober, industrious and moral. In this manner the rough sailor and lawless mutineer made himself the civilizer and teacher of a happy community, such as poets and romancers have described in their picture of the golden age.

10. It is pleasing to add that the Pitcairn Islanders remain to the present day in this state of primeval simplicity and innocence, untainted by the vices, the luxuries, the artificial wants and the social evils of the rest of the world.

---

9. What is the present condition of the Pitcairn Islanders?

CHRONOLOGICAL TABLE

OF

EVENTS IN THE HISTORY OF ASIA.

	B. C.
Creation of the world,	4004
The Deluge,	2348
Confusion of tongues at Babel,	2247
Foundation of the Assyrian Empire,	2229
Abraham's journey to Canaan,	1921
Jacob goes to Egypt,	1705
Birth of Moses,	1570
Troy founded,	1400
Tyre founded,	1245
Asia Minor colonized by the Ionian Greeks,	1044
Reign of Solomon,	1015
End of the kingdom of Israel,	729
Fall of Nineveh,	607
Capture of Jerusalem by Nebuchadnezzar,	588
Beginning of the Babylonish captivity,	588
Persian Empire founded by Cyrus,	559
Birth of Confucius,	550
Babylon taken by Cyrus,	538
Reign of Cambyses,	525
End of the Babylonish captivity,	518
Temple of Jerusalem rebuilt,	515
Reign of Xerxes,	480
Malachi the last of the Hebrew prophets,	436
Alexander invades the Persian Empire,	334
Battle of Arbela—Overthrow of the Persian empire,	331
Great wall of China erected,	246
Parthian Empire founded,	246
Foundation of the Chinese Dynasty of Han,	200
Judas Maccabæus flourished,	165
Armenia conquered by the Romans,	106
Jerusalem taken by Pompey,	63
Birth of Christ,	0
	A. D.
Crucifixion of Christ,	33
Destruction of Jerusalem by the Romans,	70
Palmyra taken by Aurelian,	270

CHRONOLOGICAL TABLE.

	A. D.
Christianity introduced into Persia,	408
Birth of Mahomet,	570
Hegira or Flight of Mahomet,	622
Christianity introduced into China,	636
Jerusalem taken by the Saracens,	637
Reign of Mahmoud of Ghizni,	1000
Commencement of the Crusades,	1095
Jerusalem taken by the Crusaders,	1099
The Tartars under Zingis Khan ravage Asia,	1227
End of the Saracen Empire,	1259
End of the Crusades,	1291
Commencement of the Ottoman Empire,	1298
Conquest of Persia by Timour,	1358
Japan discovered by the Europeans,	1400
The Portuguese arrive in India by the Cape of Good Hope,	1498
English East India Company incorporated,	1579
Usurpation of Nadir Shah,	1732
Affair of the Black Hole of Calcutta,	1756
Conquests of Alompra in Burmah,	1753
Victories of Clive in India,	1757
Hyder Ali's wars,	1780
Capture of Seringapatam—Death of Tippoo Saib,	1799
Burmese war,	1824
British war with the Afghans,	1838
Opium war of the British against China,	1840
Mehemet Ali expelled from Syria by the Allied Powers,	1840
Insurrection of the Afghans against the British,	1841
American expedition to the Dead Sea,	1847
The Punjaub annexed to the British Dominions,	1849
Death of Taou Kwang, emperor of China,	1850

INDEX,

AND

PRONOUNCING DICTIONARY OF PROPER NAMES,

USED IN THIS WORK.

A.

	Page
Ab′bas,	53
Ab-bas′si-des,	86
Abd Ul Wa′hab,	88
Ab′i-bal,	93
Ab-u Bek′er,	80
A′bra-ham,	59
Ad′ams,	227
A′dran,	179
Af-gha-nis′tan,	54
Ag′lo-bites,	57
A-grip′pa,	67
Ah′med Shah,	55
Al-ba′ni-a,	157
Al-bu-quer′que,	168
Al-ex-an′der,	147
Al-ex-an′dri-a,	85
A-lep′po,	96
A-lom′pra,	177
A-ly-at′tes,	101
Am′herst,	189
An′ti-och,	96
A-pel′les,	103
A-ra′bi-a,	72
A-ra-cho′si-a,	54
Ar′a-mites,	97
Ar′a-rat,	107
Ar′ga-li,	18
Ar′go-nauts,	158
Ar′gus,	158
A-ris-to-bu′lus,	66
Ar-me′ni-a,	107
Ar-ra-can′,	177
As′ce-lin,	116
A′si-a,	13
A-si-a Mi′nor,	98
As-mo-næ′ans,	66
As-syr′i-a,	30
Au-rung-zebe′,	167
Aus-tra′lia,	212

B.

	Page
Bab′y-lon,	38
Bac′tri-a,	166
Bag′dad,	87
Bai′oth-noy,	118
Baj′a-zet,	123
Ban′kok,	180
Ban′tam,	209
Be′dou-in,	202
Be-loo-chis′tan,	54
Bel-shaz′zar,	40
Be′lus,	39
Ben-gal′,	173
Ben-ha′dad,	97
Bey′rout,	200
Bligh,	226
Boodh,	164
Bor′ne-o,	211
Bot′a-ny Bay,	213
Bour′bon,	171
Brah′mins,	163
Brooke,	211
Bu-cha′ri-a,	110
Bud′dha,	164
Bu′gis,	209
Bur′mah,	175

C.

	Page
Ca′bul,	54
Cal-cut′ta,	173
Cal′muks,	124

INDEX AND PRONOUNCING DICTIONARY.

	Page
Cam-bo'di-a,	180
Can-ton',	126
Car-pi'ni,	116
Cash'mere,	161
Cas'pi-an,	15
Cau-ca'si-a,	157
Ca-ung Shung,	179
Cel'e-bes,	209
Cey-lon',	165
Chi Ho-ang' Ti,	128
Chi'na,	125
Ching Yik,	134
Chin Wang,	129
Chris'ti-an,	226
Cir-cas'si-a,	157
Cim-me'ri-ans,	101
Clau'di-us,	165
Clive,	173
Co'bi,	110
Co'chin Chi'na,	178
Col'chis,	157
Cole'brooke,	191
Co-los'sus,	86
Con-fu'ci-us,	127
Con-stan-ti-no'ple,	104
Cook,	221
Co-re'a,	126
Co-ro-man'del,	173
Co-ry-ban'tes,	100
Cos'sacks,	152
Cow's Mouth,	172
Cras'sus,	67
Crœ'sus,	101
Cru-sades',	70
Ctes'i-phon,	83
Cu'bo Sa'ma,	142
Cy-ax-a'res,	101
Cy-be'le,	102
Cy'rus,	46

D.

	Page
Da'ba,	197
Da-i'ri,	148
Da-mas'cus,	96
Dar'da-nus,	99
Da-ri'us,	47

	Page
Dead Sea,	203
De-jo'ces,	42
Del'hi,	163
Di-o'ge-nes,	103
Du-pleix',	171
Dweep Dee,	177
Dy'aks,	211

E.

Ed'ris-sites,	87
Ei'me-o,	218
Er'ze-room,	108
Eth'ba-al,	94

F.

Fat'i-mites,	86
Fi-ran'do,	143
Fu'teh A'li,	53

G.

Gaurs,	166
Gal'i-lee,	201
Gan'ges,	190
Gar-dan'ne,	194
Gan-gou'tri,	192
Ge-dro'si-a,	56
Ghauts,	14
Ge'lums,	197
Geor'gi-ans,	160
Go-mor'rah,	199
Gy'ges,	101

H.

Ha'fiz,	52
Han,	129
Has'tings,	173
Hard'wicke,	190
Har'id-war,	191
Ha'roun Al-ras'chid,	87
Ha-wa-i-i',	221
Heb'er,	75
He'brews,	58
He-gi'ra,	79
Her'od,	67
He-ra-cli'us,	83
Him'ma-leh,	192
Hin-dos-tan',	161

INDEX AND PRONOUNCING DICTIONARY.

	Page
Hi′ram,	94
Ho-ang Ho′,	188
Hong Kong,	136
Ho-no-lu′lu,	225
Hy′der A′li,	172

I.

I-be′ri-a,	157
In′di-a,	161
I-o′ni-a,	103
Ish′ma-el,	60
Is-pa-han′,	194

J.

Jam-sheed′,	45
Ja-pan′,	141
Ja′son,	158
Ja′va,	207
Jed′do,	141
Je-bol′,	187
Jer′i-cho,	202
Je-ru′sa-lem,	84
Jes′u-its,	132
Jews,	58
Jor′dan,	200
Jo-se′phus,	204
Ju′dah,	64

K.

Ka′led,	83
Ka-ma-ha′ma,	224
Kang′hi,	131
Kar-a-ko′rum,	114
Kau′i,	221
Kha′lifs,	80
Ki′a Ki′ang,	134
Ki′en Long,	133
Kir′guis,	109
Kot′ze-bue,	195
Ku′blai Khan,	129
Kut′tub,	166

L.

Lab′u-an,	211
La-hore′,	166
La′ma,	140
La′os,	181

	Page
Leb′a-non,	97
Lot's Wife,	204
Lyd′i-a,	100
Lynch,	199

M.

Ma-ca′o,	126
Ma-cart′ney,	185
Ma-cas′sars,	209
Mac′tan,	202
Ma-dras′,	173
Ma-gel′lan,	211
Mah′moud,	51
Ma′ho-met,	76
Mah-rat′tas,	168
Ma-lac′ca,	167
Ma-lay′si-a,	206
Ma-la′ri,	196
Mal′colm,	193
Mam′e-lukes,	98
Mant-choos′,	124
Ma′ni,	48
Ma-ni-chæ′ans,	48
Mau-ri′ti-us,	171
Mau-ri-ta′ni-ans,	85
Mas-ca-ren′has,	171
Ma-va-sa-row′a-sa,	198
Me-a′co,	141
Mec′ca,	73
Me-de′a,	159
Me′di-a,	42
Me-di′na,	73
Mer′gui,	177
Mi′das,	100
Min-da-na′o,	211
Mo′cha,	73
Mo-guls′,	123
Moor′croft,	196
Mo′ses,	60
Mus′cat,	73

N.

Na′dir Shah,	53
Nan-ga-sak′i,	142
Nan-kin′,	125
Ne-bu-chad-nez′zar,	40
Nes′sur Ud Doon,	53

	Page		Page
New Guin′ea,	213	Ros′tem,	46
New Hol′land,	212	Rus′si-a,	150
New S. Wales,	213	**S.**	
New Zea′land,	214	Sa-mar-cand′,	110
Nim′rod,	31	Sa-mar′i-tans,	66
Nin′e-veh,	37	Sam-oi′edes,	151
Ning′po,	183	Sam′u-el,	62
Ni′nus,	32	Sand′wich Isl.,	220
Nin′yas,	32	Sar′a-cens,	82
Ni′ti,	197	Sar-da-na-pa′lus,	85
Nul′lah,	191	Scyth′i-a,	21
Nu-shir′van,	49	Se-leu′cus,	48
O.		Sel′juks,	105
O-why-hee′,	221	Se-mir′a-mis,	32
O-ce-an′i-ca,	206	Ser′en-dib,	165
Om-mi′a-des,	86	Se-ri-na′gur,	191
Or′muz,	169	Se-rin-ga-pa-tam′,	174
Or′to-grul,	105	Shah-poor′,	48
O′-ta-heite,	217	Shah Soo′jah,	56
Oth′man,	86	Sha′mo,	110
P.		Shal-ma-ne′ser,	64
Pal′es-tine,	58	She′ahs,	90
Pap′ua,	213	Shi′shak,	64
Pe-gu′,	177	Sho′phe-tim,	94
Pe-kin′,	126	Si-am′,	179
Per′si-a,	44	Si-be′ri-a,	150
Pha′sis,	159	Sid′dim,	190
Phœ-ni′ci-a,	92	Si′don,	93
Phil′ip-pines,	211	So-ci′e-ty Isl.,	217
Phra-or′tes,	42	Sod′om,	199
Phryx′us,	157	Sol′o-mon,	62
Pit′cairn's Isl.,	226	So′lon,	101
Po-ly-ne′si-a,	216	Sou-tcheou-fou′,	188
Pom′a-re,	218	Stab-ro-ba′tes,	33
Pon-di-cher′ry,	171	Sun′nees,	90
Prome,	175	Su-su-hu′nans,	208
Pro-me′the-us,	157	Sym-pleg′a-des,	158
Pu-an′koo,	127	Syr′i-a,	96
R.		**T.**	
Ra′jahs,	164	Ta-boo′,	223
Ran-goon′,	178	Ta′ou Kwang,	134
Ri′ho Ri′ho,	225	Tar′ta-ry,	109
Rod′e-rick,	85	Tas′man,	215
		Te-he-ran′,	194

	Page
Tem′u-gin,	114
Tha′les,	101
Thi′bet,	126
Thym′bra,	101
Ti-be′ri-as,	200
Ti-gra′nes,	108
Ti′mor,	226
Ti′mour,	123
Tip′poo,	172
Ti′tus,	68
Ta-hi′ti,	217
Tob′olsk,	155
Tomsk,	154
Ton′quin,	181
Too-boo-ai′,	227
Troy,	99
Tuf-foon′,	181
Tur′key,	104
Turk′o-man,	124
Tyre,	93

U.

	Page
U′ral,	14
U-ru′si,	149
Us′becks,	109
Us′dum,	204

V.

	Page
Va-le′ri-an,	48
Van Die′men's Land,	213
Ves-pa′si-an,	67
Vic-ra-ma-dit′ya,	164
Vind′ha,	168
Vis′a-pour,	171

W.

Wa′ha-bees,	88
Wal′lis,	217

X.

Xav′i-er,	143
Xer′xes,	47

Y.

Yak,	18
Yem′en,	74
Yer′mak,	152
Yes-di-jird′,	50
Yung Tching,	132

Z.

Ze-rub′ba bel,	65
Zi′don,	93
Zin′gis Khan,	114
Zi-o-goon′,	142
Zo′hak,	45
Zor′o-as-ter,	47

THE END.

Printed in Dunstable, United Kingdom